# TWENTY
# COTSWOLD TOWNS

*The High Street, Burford*

# TWENTY COTSWOLD TOWNS

by

Clive Holmes

CICERONE PRESS
MILNTHORPE, CUMBRIA

Printed and bound by WBC Book Manufacturers Ltd, Bridgend, Mid Glamorgan

By the same author and published by Cicerone Press

*Cotswold Walks North* 1994
*Cotswold Walks Central* 1994
*Cotswold Walks South* 1994
*The Grand Union Canal Walk, London to Birmingham* 1996

Note: All maps in this book are diagrammatic only and are not to scale

*Victoria Square and Town Hall at Painswick*

## DEDICATION
*for Akemi*

### ACKNOWLEDGEMENTS

This book is the result of more than three years of research, in the libraries of Gloucestershire, Oxfordshire, Wiltshire, Hereford and Worcester and Bath and Avon. Without the co-operation and help of the staff of these libraries progress would have taken much longer. The gathering of material also included much exploration, sketching, note making and photographing long before any of the numerous illustrations could be made. Without the company of my wife, as with my four previous books for Cicerone Press, this would have been a much lonelier and less fulfilling task; I thank her for her support.

Finally I must acknowledge the contributions made by generations of stonemasons, builders, artists and entrepreneurs who unwittingly created the material on which this work is based.

*Clive Holmes*

COVER ILLUSTRATIONS:  
*Front,* The High Street, Burford  
*Rear right,* Sally Lunn's House, Bath  
*Rear top,* North Street, Winchcombe  
*Rear bottom,* The Fosse Way looking north, Moreton-in-Marsh

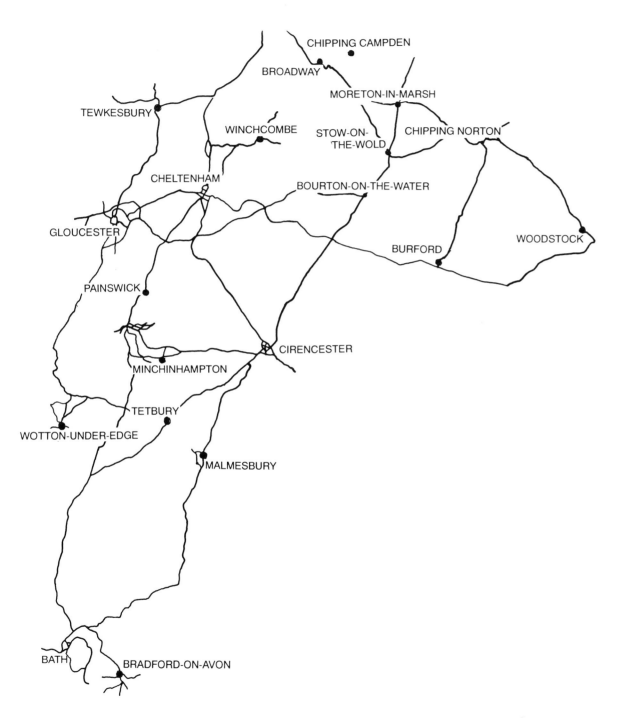

## CONTENTS

*The Redesdale Hall, the Old Curfew Tower and the stocks beside the Fosse Way, Moreton-in-Marsh*

# Introduction

I cannot claim to be a native but I do claim to be a most ardent admirer of the Cotswolds. My wife and I started to visit the area with a young family in 1973; since then we have never stopped. Further, the three years spent walking through it, illustrating and writing about it for my trilogy of Cotswold Walks, meant that we got to know it even more intimately.

The designated Cotswold area of outstanding natural beauty was enlarged quite considerably a few years ago and consists of much of Gloucestershire and part of Oxfordshire, some of Wiltshire, small parts of Hereford and Worcester and of Warwickshire. I make no excuse for straying outside this designated area because for me the most interesting and important Twenty Cotswold Towns lie roughly within an area enclosed by Broadway and Chipping Campden in the north, Woodstock in the east, Bath and Bradford on Avon in the south and Wotton-Under-Edge in the west. I make no excuse either for including in this book the town of Tewkesbury. Strictly speaking it is not in the Cotswolds and its architecture is essentially timber frame, but it is so closely connected with the Cotswolds and it has such a history that for me it is a must for the visitor to this region. Bath and Gloucester are of course cities but they are an integral part of the Cotswolds and as such are included here. Further, the visitor will find that some of those places that I call towns are to their residents still thought of as villages; I have included them here because of their size and importance.

From the earliest times the area which we refer to as the Cotswolds has been synonymous with sheep, for it was the wool and the products made from wool which gave the whole region its tremendous wealth. The very name Cotswold is said to have been derived either from the Anglo-Saxon word for sheep pen, *cote* or *code*, or an Anglo-Saxon chieftain of the same name, and *wold* meaning upland.

For centuries the wool was exported in its raw state to Europe. During the reign of Edward III, however, it became apparent that the English would do better to both produce and weave the fleece. Flemish weavers were encouraged to settle in England and the foundations of a whole new industry were in place. Soon the wool business and its allied trades came to dominate the country's economy and at its peak more than half of the national wool product came from the Cotswolds where over half a million sheep of the Cotswold breed grazed on its upland hills, each producing up to 28lb of fleece.

Vast fortunes were made by the wool and cloth merchants who in turn built the fine houses and splendid churches which we see today. Over the years a system evolved in which the merchants purchased the wool from the producer and it was then passed to the spinners and weavers who, in the main, worked in their own cottages to turn it into a thread. After this it went to the water powered fulling mills where it was thickened and shrunk into cloth.

By the late 18th century and with developments in steam power, England's main wool manufacturing facilities were developing in the north of England and time was running out for the working classes in the Cotswolds. During the following century many had left and moved north while others had emigrated; the clock had almost turned full circle.

As other parts of England developed manufacturing capabilities during the Industrial Revolution, with factories, mills, smoking chimneys and rows and rows of terraced houses to accommodate the workers, the Cotswolds became dormant and its stone buildings were little modified or rebuilt. Little changes were made by the Victorians, except to some of the churches, thus the Cotswolds stayed as it was before; its stonework becoming even more weathered. The fact that it was by-passed at this very important period of development for other parts of England meant that its appearance was unspoilt and that is why it is today such a unique part of England.

The stone of the Cotswolds, the oolitic limestone, is frequently described as being 'honey coloured'. It is perhaps this single quality which gives the region's architecture its unique appearance; sometimes almost deep golden and at others appearing as pale cream. I know of no other part of Britain where the stone has had such a profound effect on the architecture and overall appearance of the landscape as it has in the Cotswolds. It is not only the colour but the fact that when it is "fresh" from the quarry it is, to some extent "soft" and easily worked, then after exposure to the air over a long period of time it slowly hardens. It is therefore an excellent material with which to build. This is amply demonstrated by the tremendous variety of buildings which have over the centuries been constructed from the region's stone; from pre-historic burial mounds to elaborate cathedrals and from weavers' tiny cottages to grand manor houses.

Through the architecture of the whole of the Cotswolds there is an underlying similarity of style frequently referred to as "Cotswold vernacular". Before the Dissolution of the monasteries by Henry VIII these huge and elaborate buildings had required vast numbers of stone masons to care for them, but when this workforce was no longer required they took their skills to the towns and villages where they constructed solid, well proportioned, functional dwellings. The steep pitched roofs with small dormer windows, high gables and square chimneys are typical of Cotswold architecture. One of my aims in producing this book has been to put together an informative text with a series of pen and ink illustrations of what I consider to be the most significant buildings, both large and small, in each individual town, together with the most important historical incidents. A further aim was to present this information in a manner which was interesting to visitors, who may have only a short time to give to the exploration of the Cotswold towns, whilst still making it appealing and informative to residents and natives of the Cotswolds. I hope I have succeeded!

# 1: Bath

At the southern gateway to the Cotswolds stands the loveliest of Britain's cities. Described by the poet Swinburne as "England's Florence" it has, in recent years, had even more honours heaped upon it, for together with Florence and Rome, Bath has become one of only three cities in the world to be designated as a World Heritage Site. The visitor will find that Bath is steeped in history and probably has the best shopping facilities outside of our capital. Bath also has excellent restaurants, a most impressive range of accommodation to suit all tourists and, best of all, it is compact. It doesn't sprawl as do some cities. You can stroll through and around its centre rather than having to rely on transport to visit its numerous places of interest. This is indeed a bonus point for as a result of its tremendous popularity (the number of visitors is claimed to be second only to London) it has a traffic problem second to none.

The spring water that flows from the earth at a constant temperature of about 46°C and has probably done so for thousands of years gushes out in excess of a quarter of a million gallons a day. Further, it is the only hot spring in the country. Perhaps it was its temperature which many centuries ago gave it its unique appeal. The original Celts who lived in the hills surrounding this twist in the Avon valley believed it to be sacred with the goddess Sul at its source.

Legend has it that a certain prince by the name of Bladud was banished from court by his father about 500BC because he had a skin disease similar to leprosy. He was forced to wander alone tending to the swine and he is said to have observed that any deformities on their skins were gradually healed as they constantly wallowed in the hot springs. He followed their lead, bathing for long periods in the same place, and gradually he was cured. Returning to his father he related the story and so it was that the hot springs became known as a sacred place with healing properties.

As the Romans pushed westward following their arrival in Britain in AD43 a small garrison was stationed at Bath where one of their main highways, the Fosse Way, forded the River Avon. Compared to other places in this country this was quite a good place to be based as part of the invading forces. It had certain advantages over other stations, not least of all the local hot springs. The Romans must surely have felt that the gods were pleased with their accomplishments; how else would they have discovered such pleasantries in this cold,

*Bath Abbey*

6

damp land. Until they had happened upon the hot springs, being posted to this island must have felt like the bleakest outpost of the Roman Empire. Here the forests were home to vicious packs of wolves and the native people had strange practices, including painting their bodies with dyes. But they did have a goddess, Sul, who gave them this most invigorating warm water with its unique qualities. The Romans as the conquerors decided that there was much to be gained by incorporating and modifying the natives beliefs and developing the springs for their own purpose. This they did by constructing a temple above the spring in order to satisfy the Celtic goddess, and a Roman goddess who also was linked with having healing powers. Consisting of four Corinthian columns topped by a pediment with carved wings, helmets and tritons, it had at its centre a circular head with wide eyes and a handsome moustache. This became Salis to the Romans and Minerva, the goddess of healing, was to be his companion. The temple gained a sacrificial altar, while the precious water was channelled into purpose built stone baths around which a number of elegant public buildings were constructed. Over the following centuries a fine Roman town was developed probably having a theatre, forum and all the other facilities that the Romans with their highly developed form of civil-isation and skills had come to expect. In fact they developed a series of bathing places at Aquea Sulis using the two main hot springs; the main complex, however, was that which was connected to the Sulis-Minerva temple. Whilst the baths had a certain religious connection for them, the Roman people, both male and female met not just to be oiled, massaged and bathed but to relax, play games, chat and no doubt to conduct business. They could eat, drink and relax at the baths and of course they could be seen to pay respect to the gods, Sulis and Minerva.

When the Romans left Britain in AD410 to defend Rome from the invading Goths, Aquea Sulis fell into disrepair. The new conquerors, the Saxons, had little knowledge of civil engineering, sanitary systems and plumbing and Bath reverted to being a frontier post. This time it was the Saxons who held it under their leader Ceawlin following his victory at the battle of Dyrham in AD577.

For hundreds of years there was turmoil in England. Celts, Saxon and Viking fought, settled and battled again until in AD973 the first king of all England, Edgar, was crowned in the Saxon abbey of St. Peter's. The place was known as a sick person's town and by this time it was called Hat Batha. Edgar was a descendent of Alfred the Great who spent much of his time opposing the Norsemen, although to most schoolchildren he is remembered for burning the cakes whilst in hiding from the Danes between skirmishes. Following Edgar's accession to the throne peace descended on England for almost 100 years when the new invaders were the Normans.

As a reward for their part in the conquest of England the Norman Knights were given the estates of the deposed Saxon landowners. The common men were included in the package and became the serfs who owed obedience to the new Lords who held the various manors. Under this system, in 1088, Bishop John de Villula inherited the fine Benedictine priory which had by this time enclosed the hot springs of Hat Batha. Shortly after which a decision was made by the Bishop to build a huge and awe inspiring abbey at Bath. A new priory was constructed but the church was never completed. It had been intended that it would be so enormous that today's abbey would form only the nave area of the new

*Roman Bath*

7

building.

The Hospital of St. John had been founded at Bath as early as 1180 and during this period the hot springs were being looked after by the monks of the Benedictine Order entirely for the use of the sick and infirm. By the mid 13th century Bath and its religious places were in steep decline but following a visit by Henry VI in 1449, Bishop Oliver King set in motion a programme for rebuilding. William Birde was given the task of implementing the plan but as he died in 1525 the work was completed by his successor. Upon comple-

tion Henry VIII was on the throne of England and at the time of the Dissolution Bath's fine buildings were offered for sale at 500 marks to the city's citizens. The good people refused this noble offer, preferring instead to strip by illicit means the lead, glass and other materials of any value from the magnificent buildings. By the time Elizabeth I visited Bath in 1574 the abbey was in such a mess that she launched a national appeal to enable repairs to be carried out on the building.

As the reader will see, the English Civil War made a profound and grave impress-

ion on the towns in its wake. At Stowe a bloody battle was fought, at Burford the Parliamentarians shot their own men after imprisonment in the church, Gloucester had become a town under seige and poor Malmesbury had changed hands five times!

Bath was at first occupied by Royalist troops. Later the Marquis of Hertford journeyed to Wells where he gathered troops and then moved to Wales. His colleague, Sir Ralph Hopton, travelled westward to Cornwall and the city was soon occupied by Cromwell's men who proceeded to fortify it. By early June 1643 the Royalists

assembled a large army at Chard in Somerset and in a few days were but a few miles from Bath. After a couple of skirmishes the Parliamentarians were waiting for the Royalists a'top the hill at Lansdown. Thus the way to Bath was blocked. The Royalists then side stepped to Marshfield in an attempt to take the city from the north; then moved to the west to Freezing Hill. Following the early successful cavalry charges sent in by Waller, the Parliamentarian leader, the Royalists rallied and the tide of battle turned. The King's men had gained first the foot of the hill then the ridge

*The Pulteney Bridge*

but their gallant leader, Grenville, lay mortally wounded. By trickery and bad fortune the Royalists, after such gallant efforts, were pursued down the hill the following day, 5th July 1643, and eventually they were dispersed. Barely two weeks later, following a battle of Roudway Down, Prince Rupert took Bristol and Bath was held for the King by Sir Thomas Bridges. Two years later, the Royalists guarding the south gate at Bath were outmanned and the City of Bath surrendered to Cromwell's New Model Army. The city itself had suffered little during the days of the Civil War.

It was not until the mid 1600s that there was any indication that Bath's fortunes would suddenly take off. At that time "taking the waters", both drinking it and submerging oneself in it, was just becoming the fashion. The diarist of the day, John Evelyn, seems to have been one of the earliest visitors to partake of this practice but following his visit in 1654 he noted that Bath had narrow and unpleasant streets, not the best publicity for the infant spa industry. The wife of James I later visited Bath and told the tale of fire issuing from the very water in which she was immersed in the King's Bath. Greatly shocked she did not retire but transferred to the New Bath which, following the "incident", became known as the Queen's Bath. This action, together with the fact that by 1702 Queen Anne had taken her first dip at Bath, was the best publicity that the business could wish for and Bath boomed!

At the time of its emergence as a tremendous money maker the city's new industry had already acquired a mantle of rather dubious respectability; for together with all the members of society who came for various purposes, including "taking the waters", there were others who came to live off the rich. There were numerous unsavoury people from the underworld, card

players, gamblers, pickpockets, pimps and ladies of easy virtue. Amongst those who came and stayed was a rather spoilt son of a successful glassmaker who had not the will to finish his education nor to fulfil his obligations to a commission in the army which his father had paid for. He preferred the good life: drinking, gambling and women. Richard Nash lived by his wits. The position of "Master of Ceremonies", a kind of overseer post in charge of all that went on at the spa, was created at Bath. At the time of Nash's arrival this position was held by a rather brash and brawling Captain Webster. Richard was clearly a smooth talker and a person whose personality and persuasive words gave him tremendous appeal. Upon the death of Captain Webster in a duel Richard Nash was the obvious choice to succeed to his position of Master of Ceremonies. This he seems to have done with alacrity, immediately giving the city an upmarket image by introducing a number of reforms. From then on the Corporation was required to keep the city's streets in good repair and the taxi drivers of the day, the sedan chair carriers, were to have their fares regulated. No longer were riding boots or swords to be worn at front benches in the ballroom, nor were children or elderly women to sit in these places. So popular did Nash become that he was referred to as the 'King of Bath' and it was said that he crowned himself with a hat of white beaver fur. He undoubtedly amassed a fortune for himself but died almost penniless at 86 years. During his lifetime the discipline that he had imposed, and which had resulted in a much more genteel pattern of behaviour for Bath, was copied and incorporated by other towns involved in the same business.

The other great contributor to Bath at this period was Ralph Allen who was the Assistant Postmaster. He had much to do with developing a postal system for England which eliminated the need for all the

mail to pass via London. As a result of this work he became very wealthy. Ralph Allens Drive at Bath follows the course of an old tramway system which he developed for the transportation of stone from the quarries at Coobe Down to the Avon. Here the Avon Navigation Company, in which he had heavily invested, transported the stone to the city. This of course was the honey coloured oolite for which the southern Cotswolds is justifiably famous.

The architect John Wood was a native of Bath who had worked on various commissions in the north of England and in the capital city. The beauty of Bath is, in the main, of his making. It was he who had the combination of skill and vivid imagination which allowed him to develop the graceful crescents, the long rows of elegant terraces and the majestic squares which, together with the huge areas of green, garden and parkland make this city what it is. A succession of architects including his son carried on his work. Following the completion of Queen Square in 1726 by Wood himself right through to the Pump Room, which was completed by John Palmer in 1799, Wood's influence is undeniable.

Throughout its history Bath had not benefited from wool and wool products to the same degree as the major towns of the Cotswolds had. It had rather ticked along steadily. From medieval times there had however been regular employment for weavers and the residents of the former local villages that had, during the 18th century, become suburbs of Bath. This continued during Victorian times. During the early 1800s its heyday as a resort town seemed to be in decline and other down to earth industries were developed to sustain its populace. The Kennet and Avon Canal, which was completed in 1810, was followed a bare 30 years later by the railways of the Great Western, the Midland after a further 30 years, and the Somerset and Dorset in 1874.

*Beckford's Bridge, Lansdown Crescent*

*Sally Lunn's House*

Thus the industrial age was well catered for. Additionally, toward the close of the 19th century the spa image regained its former popularity and to this day Bath has never looked back but has gone from strength to strength as an international tourist centre.

As already mentioned Bath is very compact given that there is so much of such high quality for the visitor to see and enjoy. At the centre of it all stands the Abbey Church of St. Peter and St. Paul. It stands quite authoritatively, almost pure Perpendicular Gothic, on the site of the nave of the former Cathedral constructed by the Normans and dates from the close of the 15th century. It is neither as large nor elaborate as some of our cathedrals. Its plan is that of a cross and it is amply clad in flying buttresses with a tower which is bold and square. Any effect of heaviness of its exterior is easily counterbalanced by the finely serrated parapet with lightly pieced arcading which is in some way similar to the fine filigree appearance at Gloucester Cathedral. The 16th-century 'dream ladder' of Bishop King embellishes the turrets of the west front. Inside it is certainly one of the lightest and airiest ecclesiastical buildings in England, having over 50 windows.

With the altar close up to the inner east end and no screen to divide its interior the openness becomes predominant. Fan vaulting is also one of the outstanding features of the building, the oldest being 16th century. In the south transept it is about a hundred years younger and that of the nave is the most recent, being 19th century. It was during this time that Sir George Gilbert Scott carried out his extensive restoration of the building, adhering with great sensitivity to most aspects of the former design.

Most Cotswold churches are rich in commemorative tablets and memorials to those who contributed, from their wealth made from wool, to extend or modify the churches which existed during their lifetime. Here at Bath there are a goodly collection, some very elaborate and ornate but in the main they are all from the 18th century. Perhaps the one exception is the window of 1949 at the eastern end of the north chancel aisle. It shows St. Dunston, the Archbishop of Canterbury, placing the crown of England upon the head of Edgar, the first King of England, in AD973. This must surely rate as the most important reminder of the significance of the Abbey of Bath in the history of England and the traditional adherence to that very first Coronation all those centuries ago.

There can be no doubt that there is no other bridge quite like it in all of England, let alone in the Cotswolds. In my opinion the Pulteney Bridge is unique and beautiful. It has been described as a modified form of a design for the Pont di Rialto in Venice. Triple-arched and high-sided it spans the Avon with an elegance all its own and has well-proportioned shops enclosed securely down each side of the roadway. It is the only Robert Adam piece of architecture in the city and its construction was finished in 1774. The view of the bridge across the river with the weir in the foreground is one, I am sure, which makes one of those lasting impressions on the visitor to Bath. Initially it was intended to cross the Avon and lead up to a new estate development of Bathwick. The estate itself was the notion of William Johnstone who, by marriage, became a member of the wealthy Pulteney family. The Bathwick project got no further than the drawing board but fortunately the bridge became reality.

Most visitors to Bath will be aware of Sally Lunn's House in North Parade Passage. The house is said to date from the late 15th century and as such is the oldest building in the street. It has a false front with sash windows which was undoubtedly added to make it more fashionable during the 17th century. Sally Lunn was said to have been a noted cook who became well known in Bath for her cakes and pastries. No doubt she would be pleased to know that her former premises are still used as a tea shop.

Not far away and close to Westgate buildings, the house built in 1570 for Edward Clarke is one of the few buildings in the city to survive from Elizabethan times. The Abbey Church House was damaged by German bombers in 1942, since when it has been restored. Throughout its history it has been the home of a number of different families and accordingly has been known by their surname. First it was Hungerford House, then Leamington House. Later it was Savill's Lodgings, before becoming Skrins Lower House, then later it was Hetling House. When it was purchased by the rector and churchwardens of the Abbey in 1888 it acquired its present name. At one time during its history it had a pump room at the rear to which the brother of Jane Austen made frequent visits. While she always remained unconvinced as to the benefits of taking the waters he was obviously enthusiastic about the benefits. Whatever the truth may be he seems to have suffered little for his beliefs as he died at the age of 84.

*Royal Crescent*

The narrow lane Hetling Court goes through to Chapel Court where in 1180 St. John's Hospital was founded by Bishop Reginald. Due to its occupants wearing blue gowns it understandably became known as the 'Blue Alms' house. By the early 1700s the Duke of Chandos had the whole lot rebuilt in the form of a close with a townhouse for himself. The buildings were further extended in 1877.

Some distance away in the lesser known Trim Street is General Wolfe's House, the former home of the parents of one of England's most famous soldiers. By the time he was to lead the English expedition in Canada he had already acquired a considerable reputation as a general, but his scaling of the Heights of Abraham and the routing of the French armies was undoubtedly his finest and his last battle. He had lived his earlier life in Kent but came to Bath when his health was at a low ebb in 1757. The house is said to have been the work of Thomas Greenway, the warlike decorations being added later as a tribute to General Wolfe.

Trim Street is one of those parts of the city that will be 'discovered' by visitors who have time to browse and linger a little longer than those who are on a whirlwind visit. During earlier times St. John's Gate stood close to where the attractive archway with its two storied building above it now stands. The street acquired its name from George Trim who was a wealthy clothier and had much to do with the development of this part of Bath.

Even the visitor with little time to spare will want to visit Milsom Street, New Bond Street and Barton Street. Old Bond Street must not be missed either for this was a busy place, so it seems, when Jane Austen resided at Bath and parts of her books were obviously inspired by what she saw and whom she met in this fashionable city. Today Old Bond Street is a pedestrian thoroughfare, and a very pleasant stroll.

Whilst mentioning a few of the city's streets it is worth noting one of the city's foreign residents who became famous. William Herschel was a German deserter who escaped capture and settled in Bath in 1772. He was an accomplished musician and organist but at heart he was an astronomer. He lived in King Street and in 1781 he was attributed with the discovery of the planet Uranus.

At about the same time over on Orchard Street lived the Linleys who had a young servant girl by the name of Emma. She had breathtaking looks and an eye for the men. As it happened a young officer in the Royal Navy was convalescing just a short distance away and it is just possible that they met at Bath. He was Horatio Nelson and she later became better known as Lady Hamilton.

The name of Bath as a city is synonymous with squares and crescents intermingled with gardens and parks, for it is as much to see the spaces in and around the elegant architecture as it is to do with the architecture itself and the intriguing history that visitors still flock to Bath. One of the city's most famous architectural places is the Royal Crescent. It consists of 30 dwellings in a huge curve with no less than 114 Ionic columns which support an ornate

cornice reaching from one end to the other. It was the first time an architect had evolved such an unusual notion as a curved structure in this country. John Wood the Younger was said to have sought his inspiration from Rome's Piazza S. Pietro and commenced the work in 1767. Eight years later it was completed. Victoria Park complete with tea place and splendid band stand, St. James's Square, Camden Crescent, Lansdown Crescent and the large diameter of the Circus are all places to be seen by the visitor. The Circus, whilst not being the most attractive of places in Bath, is possibly the most majestic. From the top of the parapets adorned with huge acorns, through Corinthian columns, Ionic columns and Doric columns at the ground floor, it is quite magnificent architecture. Not far from the Circus is Circus Place where, in the Carriage Museum amongst other exhibits is a Bath chair used by Queen Victoria.

John Wesley had opened a school near Bristol, but in 1852 (a year after the Great Exhibition in London) it was transferred to Lansdown Road, Bath. In the early days education at Kingswood school was only for the sons of Methodist preachers but over the years entrance restrictions became more relaxed. The Perpendicular Gothic design of the building was the work of James Wilson.

With the great gusto they applied to updating many of England's churches, the Victorians also demolished buildings, one of which was the manor of Claverton which had stood since medieval times. Its place was taken by a grand mansion designed by Sir Jeffrey Wyatville. Today this mansion and its contents underline the strong connection that still exists between Britain and the New World; for it is the only real Museum of America in Europe. Complete rooms have been built using many genuine items and authentic materials which have been transported from the United States in order to provide the visitor with an insight

into the life, the dwellings, the furniture, the fixtures and fittings during the early years of life in the New World. Presumably it was felt that during the same period in England Bath was evolving as the country's most elegant city, so what better place to show how it was across the Atlantic.

I have already mentioned the baths themselves but what of the assembly rooms and the elegant pump rooms which grew up around and about this source of such a precious commodity? In 1708 it was decided by Thomas Harrison to erect the city's first assembly rooms in Terrace Walk. With formal gardens close to the river and with fine views of the surrounding hills it was described as a very pleasant morning room. Nineteen years later John Wood the Elder produced another set of rooms down in lower Bath which was called Lindseys Assembly Rooms. By 1771 in Bennett Street, Wood the Younger was building the Upper Assembly Rooms which accommodated a card room, tea room and ballroom. Damaged during the bombing of the 1940s but since restored, the Upper Assembly Rooms have been used for numerous and varied functions, while below ground is the city's Museum of Costume.

Following the publication of the treatise acclaiming the benefits of the waters of Bath by Dr. W. Oliver in 1704, John Harvey built a single storey building in 1706. This new Pump Room was a functional, practical and reasonably good looking structure but as the business developed better facilities were required. In 1784 toilets were provided, an authoritative looking colonnade on Ionic columns was added to the building, and by 1788 the Grand Pump Room was being built. Designed in the first place by Baldwin it was later enlarged by Palmer. Its North Front opens onto the Abbey Church Yard with four Corinthian columns interspaced with five elliptically shaped windows. Above, the pediment is decorated with a

wreath of oak leaves and acorns below which is the declaration in Greek that "Water is Best". The interior underwent total renovation in 1986 and provides an insight into the elegant surroundings in which the fashionable visitors and residents alike would come to take the waters, to see and be seen by those of both sexes whom they wished to impress.

# BATH

P   Parking
P.O. Post Office
1   The Abbey Church
    of St. Peter and St Paul
2   Roman Baths
3   The Roman Baths Museum
4   The Grand Pump Room
5   The Concert Room
6   Sally Lunn's House
7   Abbey Church House
8   St. John's Hospital
9   Theatre Royal
10  Cross Bath
11  Beau Nash's House
12  General Wolfe's House
13  The Guildhall
14  Pulteney Bridge

# 2: Bourton-on-the-Water

The most attractive feature of Bourton-on-the-Water is surely the manner in which the River Windrush has become such an important part of the town's centre. The Romans crossed the river here in about AD45. with their splendid road the Fosse Way, and over the following centuries several bridges have been constructed. The small bridges we see today linking the grassy banks on each side of the river were mainly constructed during more recent times although the earliest dates from 1775. The bridges are low and graceful, with stonework designed and built in a manner which fits in comfortably with the older stone architecture of the town. No wonder is it that Bourton has been called the 'Venice of the Cotswolds'.

Today the town has been developed to accommodate and cater for an unending number of tourists. Tour buses, cars and caravans jockey for positions while school parties, shoppers, and day trippers converge upon the streets, the restaurants, the tea shops, the pubs, inns and the fish and chip shops. On summer days the wide grassy verges beside the river are a favourite place for picnickers, while children squeal with delight as they paddle in the shallow waters of the Windrush.

Amongst the many attractions of Bourton and to encourage the visitor to part with his cash is the Motor Museum which is housed in the former lower mill. Here old cars, motor cycles, bicycles and die cast models are on display. Still in the High Street is the Model Railway where many hundred square feet of intricately detailed layout enhances a large collection of foreign and British train models. At the Cotswold Perfumery further down and on the opposite side of the river, the visitor can sample the perfumes, watch the blending and manufacturing of perfumes, all of which takes place on site. The Butterfly exhibition houses an unusual display of live butterflies in glass fronted cases. During recent years however, exotic spiders, chameleons and other novelties of nature have been included. Birdland, as the name implies is for bird lovers of all ages and consists of several acres of parkland in which are housed a tremendous variety of bird life, many of them free flying. Perhaps the best known attraction, certainly to the children, is the Model Village. I believe it is the oldest of the tourist attractions in the town and was probably the project which put Bourton-on-the-Water on the tourist circuit in the first place. The model village is a 1:9 scale model

*Summer evening at Bourton*

of Bourton itself, an exact replica in Cotswold stone of the town as it was between the wars. Due to its size and scale this one never ceases to enchant the children who seem easily able to relate to the buildings being closer to their own size. Some people have described present day Bourton as a Blackpool of the Cotswolds, others have likened it to Brighton without a beach, but I like to think of it more as a family holiday town set within the Cotswolds.

Obviously it has not always been so busy but a settlement of some kind has been traced back to the Iron Age where an earthwork or defensive development was constructed at the top of a slope just to the northeast of the town and was known as the Salmonsbury Camp. The natives at that time were part of the Dobunni tribes whose centre was just north of Cirencester and whose remains have been noted in and around other Cotswold towns. The site at Salmonsbury enclosed an area of over 50 acres and originally consisted of a double set of ramparts and ditches with two entrances. In plan it was square and had a spring with a stream that drained through marshland to the River Dickler, while to its south ran the River Windrush. Later, when the Romans came evidence proves that they were present in and around the town with remains being found in the form of coins and building materials close to the junction of the Rivers Dickler and Windrush. Further, it is thought that Salmonsbury Camp may have been occupied by the Romans, at least for a short time.

Much later, at the time of the Domesday Survey, Bourton is described as being under the 'bond of St. Mary's of Evesham, in Salmonsbury Hundred' and in the late 13th century it is thought that a mill of some kind was owned by the Abbot of Evesham at Bourton. During later centuries it is evident that a fulling mill was built next door to and owned by the Manor. It is assumed that it was at this time and for the purpose of powering the mill that the river was diverted in the first place, thus we can get some idea of Bourton taking its present form with the river as a centrepiece. However, the addition to the name of 'on-the-water' did not take place until the mid 1500s.

With the decline of the wool trade during the 18th century a footwear industry developed in the town which continued in strength until well into the next century. Around this time a great deal of rebuilding was taking place as the older timber framed

*The River Windrush at Bourton-on-the-Water*

dwellings were pulled down and newer stone architecture took its place. Bourton, however, cannot compete architecturally with some towns of the Cotswolds for most of its buildings are modern or have been modernised in order to cater for the tourist business. One of the buildings of interest unaffected in this way is the fine Palladian style building at the junction of Sherborne Street and Bow Lane known as Harrington House. Built and roofed in local stone, the whole thing is topped by a domed gazebo and has a balustraded parapet. The gate-posts and doorway are highly decorated, as are the windows, and at the rear a large

Venetian window lights the main staircase but this cannot be seen by the bystander. Today's house is the result of much rebuilding and development of earlier properties on the same site. Dating from the early 1700s it was modified during the mid and late 1700s, the northern part of the building being used as the town brewery a hundred years later. By 1922 Harrington House became the property of a Mr. Fort who added a southern wing and returned the whole building to a private residence. In later years this very imposing structure has become a centre for Special Interest Holidays. A few other dwellings beside the river are worth looking

out for, being old examples of true Cotswold architecture. These include in Sherbourne Street the Old Manse of 1748, now a hotel, Boxbush House which is 17th century, and Dial House of 1698, which stands to the rear of the roadway on the northern edge of the Windrush.

It is interesting to note that William Bliss, owner of the tweed mills at Chipping Norton, had much influence on the development of Bourton during the railway age. He was well aware of the benefits to be gained from a regular and efficient transportation system which would supply coal from the valleys of South Wales, with which he could

power his wool mills, not to mention the added potential for the speedy distribution of his end products. Consequently it became imperative that a route from Cheltenham to Banbury was linked to the Banbury, Oxford and London route of the Great Western Railway Company. The project was completed in four stages, the first part being to link Chipping Norton with the village of Kingham. It seems quite ironic that after the demise of the railways in Britain and the so-called axeing by Dr. Beeching in previous years, the important junction at Chipping Norton no longer exists but at the village of Kingham the station is still functioning and

trains still stop there. Such is progress! In March 1862 the next stage was opened. The railway then ran from Chipping Norton through Stow-on-the-Wold to Bourton-on-the-Water. It was called the 'Bourton-on-the-Water Railway' and became part of the West Midland Railway. Following many planning and financial problems the third stage of the route from Bourton-on-the-Water to Cheltenham opened 19 years later and after a further six years Chipping Norton was linked to Banbury. During the early years of its operation the railway was primarily a single track venture but after a number of additions an express railway ran

from 1906 until 1939 when Newcastle on Tyne was linked to South Wales, but from Newcastle to Cheltenham alone took about 11 hours to complete. The station at Bourton finally closed its doors after 100 years of operating in autumn 1962 and the track was lifted in 1965.

The Parish Church of St. Lawrence at Bourton is said to stand on the remains of a Roman building and a drain of Roman construction was unearthed during the rebuilding of 1784. Later, in 1880, when the vestry and organ chamber were being added by Sir Thomas Jackson, certain remains claimed to be those of a Roman

temple became apparent. It is known however that a Saxon church stood on the site which may have been the result of land being given in AD708 by the Saxon Cenred to the Abbey and Convent at Evesham which had then only recently been formed. It was agreed that the Abbot in return would provide monks to spread the gospel in and around the Bourton area. At that time the church would have been a wooden structure and by the time of Domesday Bourton had a priest and a church with lands totalling 60 acres. By 1110 a Norman building dedicated to 'Our Lady' had replaced the earlier one. Until the rebuild-

ing undertaken just over 300 years ago it must have been one of the oldest churches in this part of the Cotswolds and possibly in England. However due to various restoration projects the oldest parts to survive to the present day are the tiny stone crypt beneath the high altar which, it is believed, dates from the early 12th century, and the chancel built by Walter de Burhton in 1338 when the church was re-dedicated to 'St. Lawrence'.

Today's church is much as it was left by the Victorian restorers under Sir Thomas Jackson when the Gothic north aisle was rebuilt, after which the south porch followed. In 1891 the former Classical style

**BOURTON-ON-THE WATER**

| | |
|---|---|
| P | Parking |
| P.O. | Post Office |
| T | Toilets |
| 1 | The Church of St. Lawrence |
| 2 | Model Railway |
| 3 | Costwold Perfumery |
| 4 | Motor Museum |
| 5 | Birdland |
| 6 | Harrington House |
| 7 | Finden Lodge Hotel |

nave was altered to Gothic. The tower dates from the earlier rebuilding of 1784 and the larger Georgian, lead-domed capping gives it an unusual external appearance, not like a Cotswold church at all. Inside, after all its restoration and rebuilding, the most recent being in 1952, it is a pleasant and inviting church with one of the most attractive altars for many a mile.

*Above: A winter's day at Bourton-on-the-Water*
*Right: St Lawrence Church*

# 3: Bradford-on-Avon

The Town Bridge

Situated at the southernmost part of the Cotswolds, straddling the river at the eastern end of the Avon Valley, almost enclosed to the north and west by hills, Bradford-on-Avon is one of the most attractive towns in England. I must confess to a great affinity for Bradford. I like the steepness of its narrow streets that afford so many vistas over the rooftops to the river below. I enjoy the variety of its stone architecture and feel that there is a certain charming quaintness to the buildings that rise one above the other in streets which cling to the steep sides of the valley.

The town's centrepiece is undoubtedly the Town Bridge. Originally from medieval times when no doubt it was narrower, more like the old packhorse bridge near the Tithe Barn, Town Bridge was modified during the 17th century when it was probably widened, although some of the original 13th century work still remains at its southern end. On the eastern side, built over one of the piers, is a small, almost square building supported by stout stone corbels which overhang the waters of the Avon. It was known as the 'Chapel House' despite its use at one time as the town's 'lock up', having previously been a toll house. It was also called the 'Blind-house', possibly due to its shortage of window space. On top of this small and unusual building is a weather vane which depicts a fish known as the "Bradford Gudgeon".

Due to the mighty Roman city of Bath being so close there would be little reason for any major Roman settlement in or near Bradford, and while certain artifacts have been found in the vicinity there is little to support any claims that Bradford was Roman in origin.

The earliest connections are with the Saxons and around AD652, following a battle between the King of Wessex and

*The old 'Lock up' at Bradford on Avon*

*The Saxon Church of St Lawrence*

those who opposed him, the place became known as 'Bradanforda'. Following the battle a small settlement was developed near the river that had formed a natural boundary between Saxon and native Briton.

Around the year AD700 Aldhelm, who was a former abbot of Malmesbury Abbey, a learned man and a confident musician who later became the Bishop of Sherbourne, had much to do with the construction of one of the earliest buildings still standing in the town and indeed throughout the region. I refer to the tiny but lovely Saxon Church of St. Lawrence that stands in Church Street. Until 1856 little was known of its existence as it became almost enclosed by the close proximity of neighbouring buildings, and as it was partly overgrown with ivy and the chancel had become part of a three storied cottage, it was little wonder. In spite of this disguise the vicar, Canon Jones, set in motion certain steps which were to reveal to all this fine old building. Today the Saxon church is as close to its original form as is possible, given its great antiquity. It is very small in stature. The Nave measuring 25ft x 13ft has a height of 25ft, the Chancel is only 13ft x 10ft and is 18ft high, while the length of the porch is barely 10ft x 10ft 6ins x 15ft high. The Chancel arch is claimed to be the smallest in England and is only 9ft 8ins high by 3ft 6ins wide with two carvings one on each side. At the time when the Chancel formed part of the cottage the stone floor was covered by a timber floor and if, as has been assumed, the Church had been used during the Middle Ages as a charnel house, then it is unlikely that the stone floor would have been interfered with, therefore it may be from an earlier time. The small stone altar was constructed in 1970 from stones found near the church and it is felt that they may have been remnants of the original altar or perhaps part of a shrine of Edward the Martyr who was the half brother of King Ethelred. The arcading on the exterior of the

building is true Saxon and goes all the way around the building. It is worth walking round to the rear of the church just to see it.

By AD1001 King Ethelred had made a present of Bradford monastery and the manor to the Abbess of Shaftesbury but it suffered greatly at the hands of the Danes. It was probably during this period that the monastery was razed to the ground. It was also during this time and in the surrounding countryside that King Alfred and his followers fought their many battles with the Norsemen.

The huge and handsome Tithe Barn close to Barton Farm bares witness to the town's connection with Shaftesbury Abbey. The barn was built in the 1340s and is little changed since its completion when it was used as an enormous granary for the abbey. It has been likened by some historians to a cathedral, a comparison I find difficult to accept, nevertheless the barn is quite majestic and is claimed to be the finest in the southwest. Its massive stone walls measure 168ft long and the roof of stone tiles, weighing around 100 tons, is supported by huge timbers that span 33ft.

Access across the river to Barton Farm buildings and the barn were, in the past, by way of the picturesque Packhorse Bridge with its three stout piers and pointed arches. Today it is used only as a footbridge and for the visitor with time to spare it provides a means of reaching the opposite hillside from where there are excellent views across the valley.

Dating from medieval times is Barton Farm although it may go back even further, possibly to Saxon times. During the 16th century it was known as the Manor House so it is possible that parts of the building or the buildings that preceded it are earlier than medieval. The original farm covered a high acreage of land on both sides of the river and it is possible that from the farm a route ran out across Salisbury Plain which linked up Bath and the port of Bristol.

The manor of Bradford remained in the possession of the Abbey of Shaftesbury until Henry VIII dissolved the monasteries, when it passed to Sir Edward Bellindham, a Privy Councillor and soldier of renown. Being but a small town the religious changes and upheavals that took place at Gloucester and other important centres overbear to a great extent those that came about at Bradford. For instance it is not well known that some years before Henry VIII's Dissolution came into effect one of the early Protestants was burnt at the stake at the corner of St. Olave's street and the Shambles in 1532. Further, one of the town's vicars, William Byrde, lost his job (fortunately not his life) for his outspoken comments against Henry VIII and the manner in which the King was treating the church about the time of the Dissolution.

As with the Cotswolds as a whole Bradford's prosperity and development came from wool; in fact wool at one time was by far this country's greatest export and the main commodity on which England's wealth was built. Thus if you were involved with the wool business there was a very good chance that you became very rich, as many did throughout the Cotswolds. Although the wool business commenced around 1300 it reached its zenith about 200 years later. For Bradford the Tudor times were indeed good days. During the 16th century Thomas Horton became a leading member of the town's woollen business, founding a charity of his own name. He also built an aisle in the parish church, the Church House, and was responsible for the very fine Westwood Manor House just a few miles out of Bradford.

*Tithe Barn*

A fulling mill down on the River Avon in the town was owned by another member of the same family, Edward Horton who, like so many others who became rich during the centuries of booming business, took his profits and invested in land and estates when trade began to decline. The Lucas family, for instance, built South Wroxal Manor a little to the north of the town and rebuilt Staple Ashton church. But during the changes that took place in the industry there were undoubtedly periods of unrest. One of those occurred when an inspector from London, who arrived to investigate the work of the listing of cloth by the Customs officers, was thrown into the River Avon following a disagreement with the wool workers of Bradford.

In order to strengthen their already powerful position in the business the families who headed the wool trade intermarried. An instance of this is William Yerbury who married Ann Long, the daughter of another wealthy wool family. Later during the English Civil War and due to their wealth, it became important for the opposing sides to have the loyalty of these rich families. The Yerburys, it was said, were loyal to the King, and Edward Yerbury was the Commissioner for His Majesty. Unfortunately on the cessation of fighting he was fined by the Parliamentarians and had his estates compounded. He was obviously a popular man though, and his fellow clothiers of the town petitioned that he should be treated leniently. The petition did not carry much weight and Edward ended his days at far away Plymouth.

As clothing fashions changed later generations of the Yerbury family either opted out of the business developed by their forefathers or they catered for the newer markets. This was in fact the case of Francis Yerbury who was a man with a certain mechanical aptitude. He had an idea that if a technique could be developed that would enable wool to be manufactured in a similar manner to the methods used in the production of silk, then the resulting produce would be of a much finer and smoother quality. As a result of his work and experiment a fine twilled cloth was produced which soon replaced the broadcloth being made at Trowbridge; broadcloth however was still manufactured at Bradford.

It is worth mentioning here that a hundred years earlier another prominent 'wool' family, the Methuens, had much to do with the encouragement of Dutch workers bringing certain little known skills and expertise to Bradford, as had been the case at Wooton-under-Edge. Today in Church Street the former residence and workplace of these immigrants still stands. Dutch Barton Cottage is a bookshop and the Dutch Barton workplace is used as a doctors' surgery. A plaque records that this is the place where the Flemish weavers settled in 1659. Undoubtedly it was due to this injection of new skill that produced the broadcloth which in turn replaced the traditional undyed cloth on which the whole trade had been based. The eldest son of the Methuen family did not follow in the family tradition and in fact became a

*Orpin's House*

22

politician. It was mainly due to his liaison with the Portuguese that the Treaty bearing his name enabled English cloth to be imported to Portugal in exchange for Port wine. The duties agreed within the Treaty favoured this trade while placing the French wine exporters at a disadvantage, thus the English taste for Port began and has continued ever since.

Zachariah Shrapnel was yet another wealthy clothier of Bradford. He had a son Henry who preferred the army to the wool business that had served the family so well. He became an officer in the Royal Artillery, devoting much time and much of his own money to developing the exploding shell. Until he perfected the exploding shell the armies of the day had relied on firing solid lumps of metal at each other but Henry's invention provided a shell which burst, scattering small fragments of metal in all directions, thereby inflicting previously unknown damage on the enemy. His invention was said to have had a major impact at the battle of Waterloo but in spite of this he received little compensation from the government and had to settle for a mediocre pension. A mile or so from Bradford is Midway Manor, the family home, and adorning the gateway Henry had examples of his inventions fixed, together with the names of battles at which his products had contributed to victory, Waterloo amongst them.

By the end of the 17th century it was said that Bradford had around thirty mills. During this period the workers laboured for long hours in miserable conditions with little hope of improving their lot and as always friction led to trouble. In 1791 one of the town's eminent clothiers, Mr Phelps, intended to convert part of his production unit to machinery. Until then the 'scribbling' process had been done by hand but if machinery were introduced hand scribbling would be outdated and those who were thus

employed would be out of work. His home, Westbury House, was stoned by a large mob of workers and in return he and his colleagues fired into the crowd. Two adults and a child were killed and others injured but in the end the new machinery was given up to the mob and duly destroyed by them.

By the mid 1800s the trade was in decline and the workhouse was home to 400 of the townspeople. During this period the Cotswolds as a whole was feeling the pinch and Bradford was no exception. Many former workers left to join the prosperous textile towns of the north while others set their sights on the New World.

Due to the decline of the woollen industry there is little evidence of expansion during the 19th century as there was with many northern towns. Here in the Cotswolds much was left as it lay, unspoilt and unmodernised during the 19th century. As the woollen trade declined a new one was born. In 1848 Stephen Maulton bought Kingston Mill amongst other premises; no doubt disused woollen mills were readily available then at a low price and they were just the premises he wanted to start producing rubber. In the early days the Crimean War provided a seemingly unending market for his waterproof products and later the railway companies became good customers. From then until recent years the town was closely involved in the production of rubber, but the newer industry interfered little with the town's architecture. For this today's residents of Bradford must surely be grateful.

To the south of the river and close to the Town Bridge is Westbury House, the former dwelling of Mr Phelps the clothier. Later it was the home of the Bethell family. Their son Richard, the First Baron of Westbury, was born here since when the building has been known as Westbury House. It was acquired by the local council in 1911 and was put to use as offices. It is a handsome

*Easing through the lock on the Kennet and Avon Canal*

three storey building with a stone doorcase that opens on to a grass forecourt.

The building that was originally Bradford's Town Hall stands solidly beneath its clock tower at the corner of Church Street and Market Street. It is modern by Cotswold standards and dating from 1855 it has been home to the fire brigade, the police, the Midland Bank and more recently the Roman Catholic church of St. Thomas More.

In Church Street is the Abbey House. Partly 16th century it is mainly a three storey 18th century building. The older part known as the annex was the home of the Hortons during the early 1500s. Also dating from the 16th century, the Old Church House in the same street was constructed to be used for parish purposes. It was later converted into cottages and by 1873 became the town's free-school. It is a solid old building in the shape of a 'T', mainly of rubble construction. The roof is stone tiled and its interior is said to contain many roughly cut beams and a fine stone fireplace. It is recognisable to the visitor by its entrance gate of wrought iron with a handsome light above it.

Lying on the northern side of the Avon are a number of houses of 17th century origin. For instance in Market Street Nos 20-24 are good two storey dwellings with stone mullioned casement windows and other fine houses of three storeys are lower down the hill. Opposite are the Pippet Buildings with four shop fronts below them. In similar style are a number of houses in Coppice Hill but unfortunately some have been modified during recent years. Close to the Saxon Church in Church Street the visitor will see a row of cottages dating from about the same period, their pointed roofs of differing heights all stone slated. Nearby, in Newtown, the town's parish clerk Edwin Orpin resided at Orpin's House. His home was square and

*The Church of Holy Trinity*

solid and in order to avoid the window tax of 1707 two tiny openings were included between the side and centre windows at the first floor level. Also in Newtown are the larger dwellings of early 18th century with two storeys and attic windows in the front facing gables. Not too distant is the Priory Barn dating from 1470.

Bradford's Church of the Holy Trinity is said to date from the mid 1100s and its external features are little changed from then. The tower, the chancel and nave are of Norman origin but the existing tower is a 15th century building and the chancel is larger than the original one, while the nave also has been extended to form an aisle. The present sacristy was constructed as a chapel during the 16th century by a rich member of the town, perhaps a member of the Hall family. Sadly the church had fallen into a poor state of repair during its lifetime and had required major refurbishment during 1864-66. While this work was being carried out the remains of a full size effigy of a woman dating from the 13th or 14th century was found. It is generally thought that it was of Agnes, the wife of a member of the Hall family, who died in 1250. The effigy is today situated near the remains of the painted rood screen in the west end of the church. As in many Cotswold churches those who became rich by dealing in wool are well commemorated. The clothier and landowner Thomas Horton and his wife are commemorated in brass, as is their merchant's mark.

High on a hill and with a good view of the town below is St. Mary's Chapel Tory, otherwise known as the Hermitage. The Chaplain to Henry VIII visited the chapel in 1553 and made a record of his visit, and in 1670 the writer Aubrey, recording the history of northern Wiltshire, said that it was the finest Hermitage that he had come across in the whole country. By the early 1700s it had been converted into one of the

town's numerous cloth factories but during the late 1800s it was but a ruin. In 1869 a private buyer purchased the ruins with a view to restoring the building, which he did, and by 1871 the chapel was again in use.

Like most towns of the Cotswolds Bradford has a good supply of old inns. The Swan Hotel bears the date 1500 but has an 18th century exterior. It could be that this "false fronting" was added to update an older building, as is mentioned in the chapters on Burford and Chipping Norton.

The Shambles reveals the only timber framed architecture in the whole town. Whilst these dignified black and white buildings are to some extent a little light relief from the cacophony of Bradford's fine stonework, it is more than likely that they were "false fronted" during the 17th century to give a more fashionable exterior to much older stone buildings.

No visitor to Bradford should miss the Kennet and Avon Canal for it has much to do with the town's prosperity since its inception, as the wool trade did during earlier times, and for those with the time to spare pleasant walks combining river bank and canal towpath are readily available.

Work on the canal commenced at Bradford and at Newbury following the passing of the 1794 Kennet and Avon Navigation Act but it was not until 1810 that the whole enterprise was officially opened. But this, the western end of the canal, was completed earlier and was in business by 1808. Within ten years trade was booming with coal and stone among the shipments outward bound from Bradford. There were also some passenger carrying craft equipped for first and second class passengers bound for Bath. As with most of the British canal systems the Kennet and Avon was forced out of business with the development of the railways and it is only since 1984 and due to much effort from voluntary groups, the Canal Trust and the British Waterways Board that the facilities for today's waterborne travellers and towpath walkers alike are available to all.

Throughout the land the profits of the canal companies were being reduced as the railway developed. In 1844 the Wiltshire, Somerset and Weymouth Railway Company was formed with the express intention of developing railway links between Bathhampton and Weymouth. Four years later a station at Bradford was completed but it took a further nine years before tracklaying was completed. Work had been held up due to lack of funds after overspending on major building works of numerous viaducts and aqueducts, not least of all the Dundas aqueduct at Limply Stoke. To celebrate the long awaited opening of Bradford Railway link, the Great Western Railway which had acquired the railway put on a free special train to Weymouth on 2nd February 1857.

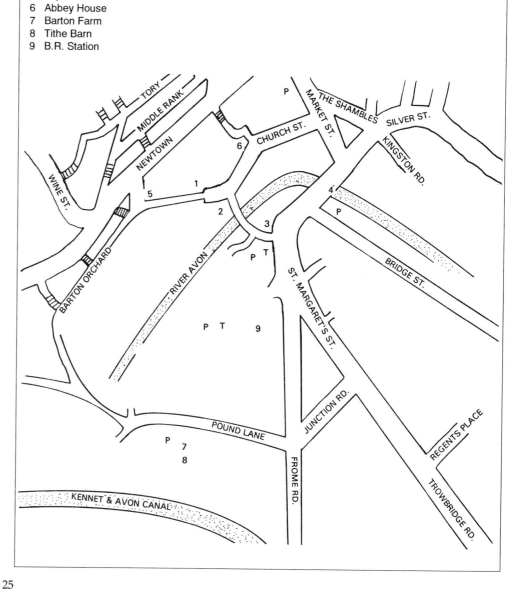

**BRADFORD-ON-AVON**

P    Parking
T    Toilets
1    Saxon Church of St. Lawrence
2    Church of the Holy Trinity
3    Westbury Huse
4    The Town Bridge
5    Orpin's House
6    Abbey House
7    Barton Farm
8    Tithe Barn
9    B.R. Station

# 4: Broadway

**B**roadway is probably the most perfect showpiece of all the northern Cotswold towns, where many of the buildings in the wide main street date back 400 years or more. It is claimed by some to be the most beautiful village in England (the residents still refer to it as 'the village'), where well-kept gardens in front of mellow stone houses, each with dormer in the roof and bow window below, reach out to the roadway, vying with each other to catch the visitor's eye. Despite the tea shops, the inns, the antique shops, the souvenir shops and the purveyors of ice-cream, Broadway has

not been spoilt in order to pander to the day tripper and the most recent additions blend in well with the original features.

In 1539 Broadway was passed to the Crown as part of Henry VIII's reformation. It had until that time been in the possession of the Benedictine Monastery of Pershore since it was granted to the Monastery by King Edgar back in AD972. However a settlement of some kind had existed at Broadway since about AD577 when following a battle at Dyrham, near Badminton, the southern Saxons ruled the area. Until it became the Crown property, it had been a tremendous asset to the Abbey providing something like a quarter of the total income. It was decided, however, to sell off Broadway in 1558 and it was bought by Sir William Babington. Unfortunately within a few years of the purchase his son was exposed as a conspirator against Elizabeth I. He and others had plotted to have her assassinated and release Mary Queen of Scots from the castle of Fotheringay. The plot failed, he was hung, drawn and quartered and his father had to sell off Broadway in order to cover the costs of his son's treachery.

Many years later the estates were inherited by the Savage brothers and they were to remain within the family for the next 200 years or so. The Sheldons, their close relations purchased the Manor and lands during the late 16th century. A century later the Winningtons acquired the Manorial rights and held them until shortly after the second world war.

Following the Dissolution of the Monasteries Broadway flourished due to its position at the foot of the great escarpment, for it was well placed between the capital, London, and the whole of the country to its west. Indeed it later became a popular staging post for coach travellers between London, High Wycombe, Oxford, Worcester and Ludlow and as a result it expanded as

*Down the High Street, Broadway*

*Entrance to the Lygon Arms*

*Near the bottom of the long High Street, the Lygon Arms*

the coaching routes became busier. Coaches with such names as Monarch, Sovereign and Wonder ran regular services, stopping off at Burford, and as travellers required overnight accommodation inns and hotels like the famous Lygon Arms (previously the White Hart), The Bell (more recently the Picton House, which today is a gallery) and a host of others developed due to this regular travellers trade. At this time in its history the coaching business provided work for numerous hotel staff, blacksmiths, grooms and all manner of allied tradespeople.

Today's visitors mainly come to see Broadway itself and today 'The Village' is still well endowed with hotels and old inns catering for all types of visitor from those who arrive on foot to those who come by Rolls Royce. The most striking of these buildings is undoubtedly the Lygon Arms which is claimed to be one of the most famous hotels in the country. There are others, of course, in other parts of England which make the same claim. The son of Earl Beauchamp, General Lygon, bought the White Hart Inn in 1826 when he also bought the not too distant estate of Springhill. He

changed the name of the White Hart to his own name of Lygon, thus the Lygon Arms was born. The Lygon Arms, as the old White Hart Inn which dates from 1620, was said to have hosted both Charles I and Cromwell, though not, I suspect, on the same evening. King Charles is also said to have been the guest of Walter Savage during 1641 at Broadway Court. General Lygon had a reputation as something of a local eccentric who had his estate planted with trees in the same formation as the troops at the battle of Waterloo in order to re-enact the battle.

As a piece of architecture of its period the Lygon Arms displays so well the gables, mullioned windows, tall rather arrogant chimneys and many of the ideal features of Cotswold buildings of the 16th and 17th centuries. The most elaborate main doorway over which the inscription reads 'To John Travis and Ursula his wife 1620' is considered to be a work of art on its own. The building was purchased in 1904 by Sydney Russell when it was in a very run down state and it was he who made the modifications and changes that have made it the fine building it is today. It has been

*Broadway Tower*

suggested that the present building stands on the site of an earlier one, possibly dating from the mid 1500s, and that the Travis door was added later. It is almost certain that a Mr White was the White Hart's landlord during this time, after which it passed to the Travis's until the late 17th century, but it is something of a mystery as to why such an imposing building should be constructed as an inn, if indeed that is what it was at this period in history.

Undoubtedly the town's position alongside the London, Oxford and Worcester route contributed a great deal to its development from the 16th century onwards. Previously the road from London to South Wales had passed through Elmly Castle, only touching the west of Broadway along Comeygee Lane, from where it scaled the Cotswold escarpment. The route followed along this old road was to a great extent already established, as to travel anywhere from the top of the escarpment it was necessary to join Ricknild Street, the Roman road which linked Wall, in Leicestershire, to Bourton-on-the-Water. There was a further important junction to the road from Coventry to Gloucester by way of Chipping Campden; thus Broadway, being tucked away at the bottom of the escarpment, right at the edge of the flat lands of the Vale of Worcester, was ideally positioned as a town through which many travellers would pass for centuries to come.

Over the years there has been a great debate as to how Broadway acquired its name. During the 10th century it was known as Bradanwege and during the following centuries it was modified slightly until more recent times when some people felt that its name was derived from the broad and wide view of the Vale of Worcester as it appeared to its many travellers from the top of Fish Hill. The name could also have come from its broad main street which had two rivers flowing down it on either side until 1862 when the rivers were run through pipes and given dipping holes at a number of places in order that buckets might be filled from them. Given that prior to 1862 both rivers had strong growths of trees beside them the development that took place along the main street was therefore to the outer edge of the rivers, the space between becoming known as the 'Broad-way'.

Throughout history the English have had many European enemies amongst whom were the Dutch. During 1797 Admiral Duncan who lived at Shipston-on-Stour was victorious in an important naval battle with the Dutch at Camperdown and as a celebration of this event Thomas Coventry, the son of Lord Coventry, supervised a huge bonfire and firework display on top of Beacon Hill. It was no doubt a very impressive sight, so much so that the sixth Countess of Coventry was convinced that a tower should be erected on the hill. Designed by James Wyatt the 65ft high folly, the Broadway Tower, was completed in 1799 and stands at the top of Fish Hill. This Gothic tower is not quite hexagonal in cross-section and to further confuse the eye it has three turrets at its corners. From its battlements

and balconies much of central England can be seen in clear weather.

In 1827 the tower was purchased by Sir Thomas Philipps who moved in with his printing press for he was mad about books and a fanatical collector. His ambition was to own a copy of every book in the world. When he left the tower and moved to Cheltenham the tower was leased to a couple of tutors from Oxford, one of whom was Carmel Price. The tutors in turn invited a number of students and friends to stay at the tower and not least among these were William Morris, the designer and social reformer, and Sir Edward Burne-Jones, the Pre-Raphaelite painter. It was said that during one of his journeys from his residence at Kelmscott Manor to Broadway in 1876, Morris passed through Burford and was appalled at the standard of the restoration work being carried out on the church. His words of disapproval were wasted on the vicar but soon after his arrival at Burford he was to write his famous letter which led to the laying of the foundations of the Society for the Protection of Ancient Monuments. He is reported to have said "Old buildings are not in any sense our property to do with as we like; we are only the trustees for those who come after us".

Shortly other prominent people of the

period were to visit Broadway, Sir Alfred Black, the botanist and landscape designer, Frank Millet, the black and white artist, John Sargent and Mary Anderson de Navarro amongst them. This great interest in the town by such painters, designers and creative people from the fields of literature, the arts and music was a tremendous boost for Broadway at this time. The coaching days were drawing to a close and due to the development of the railways, road transport had been eclipsed by rail so Broadway now turned to its architectural appeal to earn its living.

Before the first world war the town enjoyed a highly elated position as the ideal, typically English, large village in an almost perfect state of preservation. It was described as being untouched by modern developments of the period and its architectural gems were certainly sketched, painted and used for all manner of references where this imagery was required, anything from theatre backcloths to chocolate box and greeting card designs. One only has to stroll down the main street to appreciate how this reputation was earned for there are few places left which have, in spite of the continual stream of traffic and hordes of visitors, still retained the atmosphere of the past in Cotswold stone.

We are all familiar with the tragic sinking of the *Titanic* in 1912. One of the victims was the American artist Frank Millet who had resided since 1886 at the Russell House. The house was built in 1791 by John Russell and when Frank Millet arrived he modified the house to suit his way of life, including converting an adjoining barn to use as a studio.

The former Gallery Restaurant dates from medieval times and was part of the buildings, probably cottage and barn belonging to the Abbot's Grange. The Abbots Grange is said to be one of the oldest buildings in Worcestershire and

*St Eadburgha's Church*

*Now a wine bar, this small building is squeezed between the Woollen Shop and the Lygon Arms Hotel*

*The Prior's Manse was possibly the home of the Abbot's Steward*

dates from around 1320.

The Green at Broadway, just as in other parts of England, has always formed a centrepiece to the village. Here as early as 1251 the Abbots of Pershore were granted permission to hold a weekly fair and it was here that labour was hired for local work. During the 14th century badger baiting, bear baiting and no doubt many other cruel 'sports' were enjoyed upon the Green.

Behind the Green stands the Broadway Hotel, the right wing of which is timber frame while the left wing is of traditional Cotswold architecture. Originally dating from 1575 its appearance has been altered very little since 1772 except for a small forge which at one time stood in front of the right wing. Over the years the building has had a number of different uses including that of the village bakery and in 1930 it was turned into a hotel.

Up the road and close to Picton House is a row of cottages which are typical of the workers' cottages of the 16th and 17th centuries. These in fact date from around 1602 and formerly functioned as local shops, serving the residents of Broadway for many years.

The reader will recall that it was the enterprising Sydney Russell who in 1904 bought and later restored the Lygon Arms. His son Gordon excelled at furniture repairing, later developing the ability to design and manufacture fine quality furniture, and as recognition of his work he was knighted and became Chairman of the Centre for Industrial Design. The large and imposing showrooms of today's Gorden Russell Ltd. were originally two separate farmhouses, one of which has a date 1588 still on the chimney. It was known from the late 18th century as Sands Farm and was probably rebuilt during this time. During 1916 it had a two storey porch added and was completely restored by the Russells.

Until about 1850 St. Patricks of Broad-

way Tea Room was the vicarage and on the vacating of the building by the vicar the house was sold. The left gable, having a damp problem, was shingle clad while the opposite gable is of stone. Since then it has functioned as a school house, then as a hairdressers but since the 1930s has been a tea shop.

The Picton House is a fine example of a well-proportioned building of its period. It was built around 1700 as a private dwelling but by the mid century had become 'The Bell', a coaching inn. For a time it was used as a school, then it was purchased in 1830 by Sir Thomas Phillips (of Broadway Tower) who gave it its name after Picton Castle in Pembrokeshire, South Wales.

The two charming old thatched cottages, one of which is dated 1608 and are now shops, are surely the last survivors of the many that in days gone by housed most of Broadway's working population.

The large building across the road and further up the hill from the Lygon Arms is another fine example of 17th century work where the shield boldly announces '1659 - 1660'. It is known today as the Tudor House, the home of H.W. Kiel's antiques. Earlier in its life it was the Angel Inn, then a school (Burford seems to have had a leaning toward education) and later it was turned into a private dwelling. The original Mr Kiel was a cabinetmaker who worked for Gorden Russell Ltd. but started his own business here before the second world war. Tudor House is certainly a handsome building of five storeys, with high pointed gables, stone mullioned windows and a roof surmounted by tall chimneys. The adjoining building was erected in 1774 as indicated above the archway. At first it was the Bell and Crown Inn and later it was used in part as yet a further school. The large round clock was attached to the wall to commemorate the Golden Jubilee of Queen Victoria in 1887 and was renovated in 1953.

During 1907 Kathleen Adams came to Broadway and started her business in the building known today as the Bindery Gallery. She developed a reputation as one of this country's foremost craftpersons and worked exclusively for the most selective publishers. As with many fine quality, hand produced objects the market for this standard of work faded between the wars and she vacated her bindery in 1926.

At the corner of Leamington Road is one of the oldest houses in Broadway, the Prior's Manse. It dates from about 1320 and was probably built for the steward to the Abbot of Pershore. It has a rather 'ecclesiastical' front door with a protruding gable end which was added about 300 years later. Until the late 1800s the Manse still retained its own attached barn. The doorways into the barn have long since been blocked up but are still visible from Leamington Road.

Near the top of the village is one of Broadway's most famous houses of the Edwardian period, Court Farm. It was originally two separate farms, Bell and Court. Madam de Navarro, the actress, lived at Court Farm from 1893 and Maud Valerie White, the pianist and song writer, lived at Bell Farm. When she vacated her home a music room was erected thereby joining the two former farms together for the Navarros. During its heyday it was certainly the place to be invited to, as were many of the rich and famous politicians, musicians, writers and royalty during the last century.

Broadway has two churches. St. Eadburgha's Church dates from around AD1200 and has fortunately not had to endure restoration by the Victorians. It is a simple and straightforward Early English Gothic church with a central tower, a 12th century chancel and a transept dating from

*Cottages "up the hill", at Broadway*

the 16th century. The pulpit and alms box are about 100 years older. St. Eadburgha was a grandchild of King Alfred and was the Abbess of St. Peter's at Winchester. Some of her bones rest at Pershore Abbey. Generally it is thought that the reason the church is so far from Broadway was that it was positioned close to the ancient route between Wales and London, for at the time of its erection this was a dangerous route to travel and those who did so no doubt found comfort in the church's presence below the great escarpment. When St. Michael and All Angels Church was built a short distance from the Green just over 150 years ago it was generally thought that the old church would be demolished but, led by Sir Thomas Phillips, those who were opposed to seeing this fine old building being reduced to rubble eventually gained a reprieve for the building and in the main it appears today much as it did over 200 years ago.

In my early paragraphs on Broadway I mentioned the Sheldon family who purchased the Manor and the lands of Broadway during the late 16th century. They were a very rich family whose roots were at Sheldon near Birmingham. They also owned land and a mansion close to Shipston-on-Stour. As with many powerful families of their time they intermarried with other families of like status in order to increase their wealth and control. An example of this practice is the case of Ann Sheldon whose first husband was Francis Savage and whose family home was at Elmely Castle. Shortly after his death she married Antony Daston whose family owned Dumbleton. She resided at Broadway Court, not a great distance from St. Eadburgha's church, until her death at 91 years in 1619. Unfortunately Broadway Court, which must have been a very grand house when the family were at their peak, was demolished in 1773 but the old gatehouse still stands. Known as The Court, this was also in a ruinous state until 1898 when it was enlarged and restored by Sir Guy Dawber. Over the door of the old gatehouse are the crests of the three families. The reindeer was the Savage crest, the mailed fist was the Daston crest, and the one in the centre with the sheldrake was the Sheldon crest.

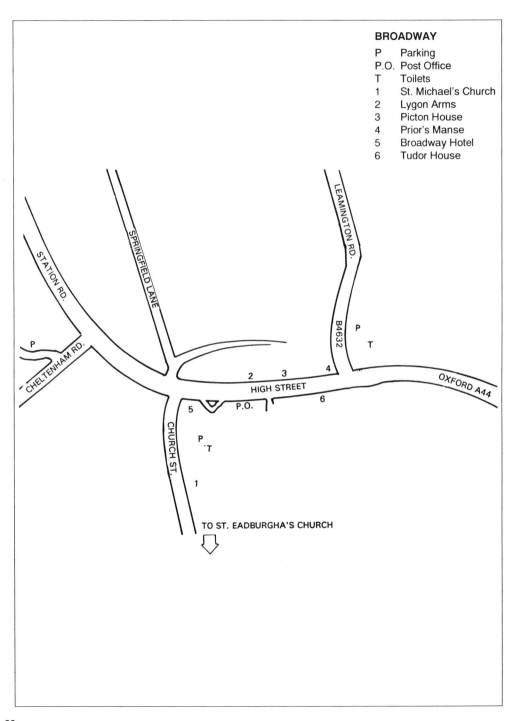

**BROADWAY**

P    Parking
P.O.   Post Office
T    Toilets
1    St. Michael's Church
2    Lygon Arms
3    Picton House
4    Prior's Manse
5    Broadway Hotel
6    Tudor House

# 5: Burford

*The fourteenth century
Almshouses near the church*

The charm of today's town of Burford is greatly enhanced by the presence of the River Windrush at the bottom of the High Street. In days gone by the river was the very reason for Burford's existence as it was here that travellers were able to ford the river and naturally with time a settlement developed. By Saxon times Burford was known as a 'Protected place by the ford' or 'Ford by the hill' and by the time of Domesday, due to its close proximity to the river, Burford had grown in size and consisted of about forty families, a simple church and at least one mill along the river bank.

Before the end of the 11th century Robert Fitzhamon held the Manor of Burford and it was he who granted the earliest charter which gave the right for markets to be held in the town. Thus the 'green light' was shown to the inhabitants encouraging them to develop as a trading community and by the 13th century a borough court existed. During the next two centuries the town had spread higher up the hill and fine houses began to reflect the steady growth in the prosperity of the town's residents.

In 1617 the Lordship of the Manor of Burford was bought by Sir Lawrence Tanfield who ten years earlier had become Chief Baron of the Exchequer. He was, it seemed, a man of great ambition and had risen to a position of power and wealth by a combination of corruption and selfishness. He was quick to see a means of furthering his aims by bringing a writ against the Burgesses who had previously governed the town with a certain prestige and individual flourish. The writ stripped them of the powers of day to day government and as the town's Burgesses had no documentary evidence to support their position they were no longer able to govern as a body. Consequently they were reduced to administering their own properties and lands of the guilds. No doubt 'helped' by the recently downgraded Burgesses the citizens of Burford were encouraged to believe that the Tanfields were wicked people, so much so that word was spread that Lady Tanfield was a witch. When she died it was said that she flew above the town in a chariot which was on fire and the vicar was called to act on behalf of the townsfolk. The story goes that he caught her evil spirit in a bottle and pushing the cork in tightly to seal her inside he threw the bottle into the River Windrush, close to the old packhorse bridge.

*The church of St John the Baptist beside the river*

Thomas Castell was in 1761 Burford's 'coaching king', for he developed the coaching routes to the surrounding towns and cities. At the peak of Burford's coaching days 40 coaches a day would clatter down the High Street. The town became well known as a centre for the traveller and coaches with such grand sounding names as the Gloucester Royal Mail, the Regulator, the Magnet and the Mazappa linked Burford with Hereford, Oxford, Cheltenham and of course London. Thus, the town became something of a transport centre for the region and a popular staging post. As a result of this new inns and hostelries sprang up to offer the traveller the facilities to be encountered elsewhere.

During the mid 19th century, just as the canals had done before them, the development of the steam locomotive enabled the railways to change the fortunes of many of the towns and villages throughout the land. The railway line from Oxford to Worcester was opened to traffic in 1852 and understandably was routed along the valley of the River Evenlode. As a result it passed not through Burford and along the Windrush valley but through Shipton-under-Wychwood, a few miles away, and on through Chipping Norton. As a result very little development took place at Burford compared with the growth of the town of Chipping Norton, at this time. The latter became something of a local railway junction. This in turn helped in the expansion of the town's industries and is reflected in the town's architecture. Burford on the other hand retains, in the main, its architecture from earlier times, unspoilt by the developments that overtook numerous other places during this period in history.

The leading townsfolk were however not concerned so much with the architecture of their town and it is doubtful whether they were as appreciative of it as the visitor to today's Burford. They would have been as keen as any to develop a railway terminal of their own or even just a railway station if that's what it took to increase their commercial opportunities. Indeed during the early 1860s quite determined efforts were made by the town's leading citizens to create a railway which would benefit the town, just as the railways were seen to be benefiting other towns. It was proposed that the Cheltenham and Oxford Direct Railway should have a station at the top of the hill and the *Oxford Journal* of the day published a list of names of the residents who supported the proposals. Unfortunately or otherwise nothing came of the project and within a ten year period it had died a natural death and Burford was spared the exposure to the railway age.

The appeal for today's visitors comes not from recent generations but from much earlier times. While the ground floors of the buildings in the High Street are a mixture of antique shops, hotels, jewellers, tea shops and souvenir shops the upper storeys are an array of limestone and timber frame buildings, some even combining a stone ground

*The Old Vicarage*

*The Old Bell Foundry, Witney Street*

floor with a black and white upper storey. The trading fronts at street level are broken at times with different doorways and old archways which facilitated the way through for wagons and coaches to rear yards and stabling accommodation. There are a variety of window frames, tall, narrow, broad, short, mullioned and metalled. Some of the buildings have false fronts given to add a more elegant and fashionable exterior to an older building during the 17th and early 18th centuries. Much of this work in the town is attributed to Christopher Kempster who during his stay in London no doubt saw many such flat façades built into older buildings. Upon returning to Burford he is said to have introduced this practice to the rich and fashion conscious of the town.

This abundance of historical architecture which justifiably makes Burford so popular is not just confined to the High Street or to its upper section known as The Hill. In Witney Street, for instance, stands the Great House, which in 1685 was described as a 'tenement being in possession of Mr. Robert Glyn'. With its rectangular outline and tall rectangular sash windows, circular windows in the attic and elliptical ones in the basement it is certainly a handsome building. The main doorway is centrally placed at the top of a flight of semi-circular steps and the Great House competes with the Rectory and the Old Vicarage as Burford's finest building. It was Christopher Kempster once again who, having worked with Wren to rebuild St. Paul's and other buildings in the capital, is said to be the builder of Burford's Great House.

Across the road on the north side of Witney Street are the remains of the Old Bell Foundry. Bell casting was once an important industry for the town and the remains now preserved are one of the buildings formerly used for this work and are thought to date from medieval times. Additionally Witney Street houses an interesting collection of cottages and old inns.

The Tolsey is an unusual medieval building seeming to stand on elephant legs and it was here that the tolls for trading rights and for fairs held in the town were paid to the merchants guild. The first mention of the Tolsey's existence is on a bill dated 1561 when the building was known as the Court House, where the town Burgesses met to settle disputes. At the rear of the building was a prison known as Blind House, the door of which is in today's Museum. From 1800 until 1956 the ground floor of the Tolsey was enclosed and was used to house the town's fire tender.

Sheep Street, just past the Tolsey, is also worthy of a mention. On the left are the offices of the *Countryman* magazine, formerly the Lenthall Temperance Hotel, beyond which is a part timber framed dwelling which is about 500 years old. This is typical of a number of houses in the town at that time. Others have at some later date had the upper storey of timber removed

*The Great House in Witney Street*

*The tremendous variety of architectural styles of Burford's High Street, as seen from Witney Street*

and replaced with stone. The former house of the hated Lawrence Tanfield is across the road: the Bay Tree Hotel was certainly a fine house of its time. Evidence exists that Elizabeth I visited Burford, as indeed she is said to have visited so much of England, but in Burford it is almost certain that she would have stayed here at the home of her most eminent politician. Further along is one of Burford's oldest inns, the Lamb Inn. Complete with some of its masonry dating from medieval times, it has functioned as an inn since the mid 1800s. The Old Brewery, situated between them, still has a 15th century malthouse and it is assumed that it was built to brew ale for the Lamb Inn. During the 19th century it was updated by the introduction of a steam engine to speed up production but it ceased to function as a brewery in 1969 and was up for sale again in 1994. Today it is the Tourist Information Office.

Priory Lane takes its name from the former 16th century Priory, but much earlier a small monastic foundation, the Hospital of St John, stood on the site and it is felt that this dated from about 1226. During the 16th century it was closed by Henry VIII, as were all other such establishments. The King then gave the priory to Edmund Harmon, his surgeon. In turn Sir Lawrence Tanfield

*The Old Tolsey*

acquired the building and extended it into a large home and later again, Speaker Lenthall of the Long Parliament, just before the outbreak of the English Civil War, lived here. He in turn enlarged it even further and added a chapel. Little of the original building remains, though, and following restoration earlier this century it became the property of an enclosed order of nuns in 1947.

It goes without saying that a building such as this with such a varied usage by such a notorious collection of residents should be expected to have unexplainable reasons for things going 'bump in the night'. Some say that a little brown monk haunts the priory and one of its earlier owners firmly believed that it was so haunted that until it was returned to the church it would always remain so. During the early hours of the morning when medieval monks were awake for their night time devotions ringing bells and singing choirs are said to have been heard. Further, the little brown monk has been seen, it is claimed, in different parts of the priory by the residing nuns.

The best time to get the feel of Burford is in the early morning before it becomes clogged with traffic, as it always does, being busy with visitors for most of the year. Walk up the High Street to the top of The Hill, turn and admire the view down the High Street to where the Windrush flows beneath the fine old Burford Bridge with the truly English landscape beyond.

At the bottom of the High Street, just to the right of the narrow bridge, are some lovely old cottages known as Simon Wisdom's Tenements. They were built by this very benevolent gentleman as part of his endowment to the Burford Grammar School. The cottages have for many years been covered in creeper but if you are visiting the town when the leaves are dead then it is possible to read the inscription on the plaque, "Alderman, the firste founder of the schole in Burford, gave these tenements wythe other to the same schole in A.D. 1577 and newly Reedyfield and Byfoled the same in 1576."

Close by is the entrance to Ladyham, which means 'Our Lady's Field by the Water'. This beautiful house, the home for centuries of the wool merchant family the Sylvesters, was more recently owned by Sir Compton Mackenzie, the prolific author who was perhaps best known for his comedy *Whisky Galore*. He had rented part of the house in 1904 for £14 while studying at Oxford and had intended to use it as a kind of monastic retreat in which he could test his ability as a writer. It was at that time two separate houses and when the last of the family who owned it drowned in the river, Mackenzie bought it for £1,400 and joined the two buildings together. This magnificent building was on sale again more recently, the asking price being £750,000.

Back in 1175 there stood at Burford a simple church of Norman construction, but on entering Lawrence Lane from the High Street it is obvious that the former simple

*Burford Bridge*

church has, over the centuries, acquired a certain air of beauty. To the best of my knowledge the Church of St. John the Baptist is the only church in the Cotswolds and one of the few subjects painted by the northern artist L.S. Lowry which where not in or close to the north of England. He painted as he saw it from Lawrence Lane in 1948, calling it simply 'Burford Church'. He added cottages to left and right of the lane more reminiscent of those dwellings of the mill workers of the northwest with which he was so familiar. Near to the church are some 14th century Almshouses. Inside the

*Cottages near the top of The Hill*

church it is obvious that as the fortunes of the medieval wool traders developed, the church was added to and improved over a period of about 300 years. In fact so much development went into the tower in the form of masonry plus 300 tonnes of bells that the graceful curving Norman arches had to be 'built in' to reinforce and strengthen the structure. This work is clearly visible from the base of the tower. Most of today's church dates from the 12th century but in the south wall of the tower stairs, below the roof of the south side, is a carving which is thought to date from around AD1000. It depicts the pagan god Epona as part of a horse with two males. Such pagan figures were frequently incorporated into the early Christian churches by the Saxons and therefore this could mean that at least parts of the tower are of Saxon origin.

Much of the Cotswolds saw a lot of action during the English Civil War and Burford was not without its share of the drama. On 13th May 1649 soon after the execution of King Charles I a group of dissatisfied Roundheads reached Burford. They had travelled from Salisbury by way of Marlborough, Wantage and Abingdon and were destined to be sent to Ireland but

they had refused to obey further orders until their grievances had been settled. Their main complaint was that they had not been paid and while Cromwell who was close on their heels was not entirely unsympathetic, he was aware that his armies had given him trouble for similar reasons only two years earlier. The mutineers had, it seemed, attempted to negotiate through intermediaries and were given assurances that no further action would be taken against them until all possibility of negotiation had been exhausted. However they were subsequently overpowered by Cromwell and his trusty Fairfax after a short skirmish which resulted in 340 troops being taken prisoner.

At Burford the only place large enough to accommodate them was the church and so these unfortunate mutineers were imprisoned in the church for three nights. During this time, no doubt to while away the time, one of them, Anthony Sedley, carved his now famous initials on the inside of the font. When 17th May dawned, the ringleaders Corporal Church, Cornet Thompson and Private Perkins were taken outside and shot as an example to the remainder who were obliged to watch the

*The Lamb Inn*

execution from the roof of the church. Today a small tablet to the left of the church door is a memorial to those mutineers.

Inside the Church of St. John the Baptist the visitor will be well aware of the tombs, brasses and memorials, not to mention the tomb of Sir Lawrence and Lady Tanfield with, perhaps fittingly, a skeleton beneath their bed, but a further item of interest is the turret clock. Hercules Hasting, a forefather of Warren Hastings, was an eminent clockmaker during the late 17th century. He resided in the town on the corner of Swan Lane and at the age of 24 years he made a new turret clock for the church. It was of similar design to that made by Clement in 1671 which is now in the Science Museum in London. Hastings had his clock installed in the tower of the church in 1685 where it stayed until 1949. Its mechanism was housed in the ringers chamber with the pendulum swinging below the floor. Since the early 1980s the clock has been powered by electricity; previously someone with strong lungs had to climb the staircase every day to wind it up.

*Early spring on Sheep Street*

**BURFORD**

| | |
|---|---|
| P | Parking |
| P.O. | Post Office |
| T | Toilets |
| 1 | Church of St. John the Baptist |
| 2 | Almshouses |
| 3 | Priory |
| 4 | Burford Bridge and Simon Wisdom's Tenements |
| 5 | The Old Vicarage |
| 6 | The Tolsey |
| 7 | The Museum |
| 8 | The Old Bell Foundry |
| 9 | The Former Brewery (TIC) |
| 10 | The Bay Tree Hotel |
| 11 | The Lamb Inn |

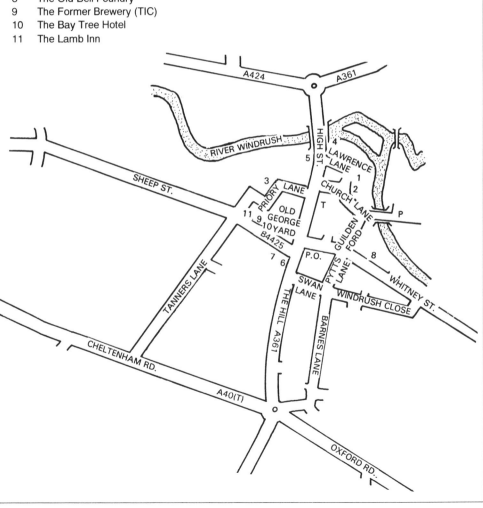

# 6: Cheltenham

St Mary's Church

It could be argued that Cheltenham has no right to be in this book as, strictly speaking, it is not in the Cotswolds. It is, however, adjacent to the Cotswolds, sitting easily as it does between the two great hills of Cleeve and Leckhampton. Superb views of the town are readily available from both. From Cleeve Hill the town is distanced with the racecourse in the foreground, and from Leckhampton Hill the view is almost the same as if it were viewed from a low flying aircraft. It was from the latter hill, famous for the Devil's Chimney, that left-over monument to generations of quarrying, that the beautiful honey coloured stone of inferior oolite was excavated. Quarrying on a serious scale commenced in 1793. The easily worked stone was used as facings for most of the town's noblest architectural masterpieces. During the peak building period a tramway carried the stone from Leckhampton down to the huge building site in the valley below, but all is quiet now on the surrounding hills except for the wind in the grass and the birds in the trees.

I often wonder if the quarrymen of old would recognise the town to which they contributed so much over the generations. Today the skyline has a goodly show of high rise buildings and offices but still prominent are the spires of a number of the town's

churches. In 1973 much of the town centre was designated as a conservation area and since then a great deal of work has been carried out refurbishing and replacing the ravages of time that have taken their toll of the former smooth skinned, Cotswold faced buildings of Cheltenham.

It is generally accepted that during the mid 700s there was a Saxon settlement near a stream and close by the foot of the Cotswold Hills where a track ran between Gloucester and Winchcombe. The place was known to the later settlers as 'Chelt', the forerunner of the name of today's town. The well-drained land was sandy and an ideal place to farm and develop. It seems that the Bishops of Hereford and Worcester both had claims to the revenues of a nearby monastery during the late 700s but like numerous other religious places of the period it was probably destroyed by the Danes during the 9th century. By the 11th century no fewer than five watermills were operating along the river.

By the time of Domesday 'Chinteneha' had become a Royal Manor with a church, which was probably the church which was

*Regency Terrace and the Neptune Fountain on the Promenade*

superseded by the medieval Church of St. Mary's. Since, by Cotswold standards, Cheltenham is quite a modern town with only limited connections with the early past, it is worth mentioning that just about the only connection with medieval Cheltenham is in fact at St. Mary's. Here 12th century pillars support the tower arches together with the two buttresses outside the western end of the church. During the 12th century St. Mary's was an acquisition of Cirencester Abbey. At this time Cheltenham was a farming town but with the granting by Henry III in 1226 of the right to hold the Thursday market its status developed somewhat and by 1313 it had become a borough. Any remains of the former market buildings were cleared from the High Street, along which the town had developed, toward the end of the 1700s. In the parish churchyard, set into the pathway of the southeast corner, were three brass measuring lengths, these were once used to check the correct lengths of traded goods at the old town centre market.

Cheltenham continued rather insignificantly to live as a market town and it was not until 1589, when William Norwood leased the Manor of Cheltenham, that the town had anyone with any specific interest in its well-being or its development.

*Amidst flower beds, trees and shrubs, the elegance of Lypiatt Terrace*

The town's prosperity continued to be based on agriculture and the marketing of its produce well into the 16th century when brewing and indeed tobacco production were being developed. Later Cheltenham and Winchcombe became the short lived centres for English tobacco growing but it was not until the discovery of the medicinal waters at Cheltenham, and with the later development of this major industry, that the town's fortunes really took off.

Close to the old parish church was a field in which, so the story goes, pigeons were seen to frequent a natural spring which had a salty deposit. The birds obviously enjoyed pecking at this deposit, so much so that a few local people started to taste the water too. They found it to be agreeable, some folk even claiming that it gave relief to those who suffered from rheumatism, constipation and gout. The fortunate owner of the field was a William Mason who enclosed his newfound source of income with a timber structure and charged a small fee for the water that was consumed. Mr Mason had a daughter who met and married a former sea captain by the name of Skillicorne and it was he who did most to give the new business a bright and sparkling image. He started by installing a pumping system, then building an assembly room, and during the latter half of the 1700s he was bottling and selling the water to consumers well beyond the town. By this time an avenue of elms linked the church and the well, which became known as Well Walk.

Here then were the beginnings of the town's boom period but these happenings on their own were barely enough to sustain this new growth industry for there were other spa towns in the process of developing in various parts of the country. For Cheltenham it was a great slice of good fortune that the ailing George III, in 1788, spent five weeks sampling the waters. At

first the King had appeared to benefit from his time at Cheltenham but shortly after his return he suffered a relapse. Whilst in the long term the 'waters' had done little to cure his biliousness and related medical problems his visit did much for the image of the town and its now quite famous product. The water source became known as Cheltenham Spa and the word "Royal" became associated with the town.

About this time one of the town's earliest building developments of any importance took place. It seemed that any town, especially if it was to be a 'spa town' - and the reader need only look at the other spa towns for clarification - simply had to have at least one Crescent. At the time it was almost obligatory. Cheltenham's was designed by C. Harcourt Martin, a man with much experience for he had already completed the very prestigious Sydney Gardens in the beautiful city of Bath. Externally the Crescent is quite a plain, simple and straightforward piece of design without the fuss of pilasters and porticoes, while inside the layout of the dwellings is far better than some of the town's houses that date from later periods.

Soon the aristocracy was visiting Cheltenham Spa in increasingly large numbers in order to "take the waters". The large numbers of visitors were a good cross-section of the richest people in the land including Dukes, Marchionesses, Earls, Bishops and Lords, and this was during the early 1800s when England was an extremely rich nation. With this huge amount of wealth circulating within the educated classes and with their appreciation and understanding of successful classic periods in history, e.g. ancient Greece and Rome, it was understandable that architecturally these periods should become influential in England. Many of those who had wealth had also enjoyed a full and rounded education. They had travelled abroad, they had

an appreciation of art, they enjoyed music and literature and above all they could afford to live the good life.

With the passing of the Enclosure Act during 1801 and in spite of the hardship it wreaked on the lower classes who earned their living from the land, it did free much land around the outskirts of the older centre of Cheltenham for development. Henry Thompson, a banker, was one of the earliest speculators, purchasing over 400 acres within a three year period. At Vittoria House, formerly Hygeia House, he opened

*Hardy's House*

a spa and a few years later he had a pump room at Montpellier Spa. Later again in 1817, with G.A. Underwood as the architect, he built a new flat roofed pump room with a Doric colonnade. During more recent times this has been occupied by Lloyds Bank. The Imperial Promenade was another development by the same architect. Constructed over a two year period from 1823, it was later described as being as elegant in appearance as the Louvre and is felt by most to equal any piece of architecture in Europe. This superb piece of terracing is brick built with a stucco facing, which was popular at the time as it was slightly cheaper but equally pleasing as an alternative to stone. At the centre of the terrace is a set of seven houses all used as Municipal Offices since 1914. The Promenade at Cheltenham, with its triple tree clad avenues, is as impressive as any urban development in the country. It runs from the Queen's Hotel to the shopping precinct in the High Street known as the Colonnade, where the road narrows causing an exaggerated appearance of length when viewed from the hotel.

In 1838, when it was completed, the Queen's Hotel was the largest in the country. It is a huge piece of Greek revival architecture with thirteen bays and it is said that during later years when the railways of Britain were vying with each other for prestige a number of their hotels were based on this design. It stands on the site of one of the earlier spas. An extra feature lavished on this part of the town is the very elaborate Neptune Fountain in Portland stone. This was erected just before the turn of the century and depicts Neptune being drawn by seahorses.

In 1824 J.B. Papworth was planning the Lansdown Estate to a "picturesque" format. It was in fact only partly completed but nevertheless it was certainly unique at that time, having dwellings set out between gardens and formal avenues of trees. As a result of his very capable designs the semi-detached home was to become an integral part of future housing developments. Joseph Pitt, a lawyer of the time, also bought land in the Cheltenham vicinity. Encouraged by the success of others with entrepreneurial skills, he intended to develop a completely new spa area at Pittville, which, if large and sufficiently lavish, could bypass even Cheltenham itself in popularity. He planned for 600 houses within 100 acres of parkland consisting of gardens, lakes and tree-lined avenues, all dominated by a large colonnaded pump room which was to be surmounted by a large and most impressive dome. To this day this Pump Room is accepted as being Cheltenham's finest Regency building and is based on the Temple of Ilissus of ancient Athens. It was designed by John Forbes in 1825 and took five years to construct. It is in every way a superb example of the classic Greek architecture of the town. Here people promenaded in the surrounding Pittville Parkland and were seen to do so during the "season", which lasted from May until September. Inside, the health giving waters were served at the pump room on the first floor while above was a library, a billiard room and a reading room. It also contained an assembly room which was designed to cater for special concerts and balls. A further example of his work in similar style is at Pittville Lawn. Here the Dorset Villa is a most elegant and lavish example of Greek Revival architecture with fluted Ionic pilasters to the front and south elevations of the building. This is Cheltenham at its very best.

Not too distant is Clarence Square where elegant Regency terraces look out over colourful gardens while the Church of St. Paul's, modern by Cotswold standards, is yet a further example of this fine architect's ability to base design on classic Greek style. This church was probably the most

*The Queen's Hotel*

recent to be built within the diocese of Gloucester during the 19th century and is a fine example of the Victorian revival church.

The Rev. Francis Close did much to promote a new form of learning; a learning that should, whilst absorbing the teaching of the Christian faith, be aware of the values of those who imparted this knowledge. So it was that his movement for the development of learning for all classes resulted in the formation of the Cheltenham School of St. Paul's College. St. Paul's College was designed by S.W. Daukes and was opened in the mid 1800s. The Rev. Close insisted

that this place of learning must be neo-Gothic in its conception and so it is, almost to the extreme. It fulfils all the requirements from its battlements, its turrets, its triple lighted traceried windows to its pointed arched doorway above the main gate. This is a classic piece of English architecture which would not be out of place in any part of England and yet it is barely 150 years old.

Unfortunately the fashion for "taking the waters" was becoming less popular by the time the Pittville development was under way and much of what was planned never got further than the drawing board but that which was completed was certainly

most elegant.

During this period of development, not only in Cheltenham but in a number of other towns and cities of England and not least in London, the love affair with what was seen as the perfection of classic architecture reached its peak. Stuart and Revett the architects published drawings of the works of Athens after which their studies were used again and again as references for architectural subjects in preference to the previously preferred Roman references. When Lord Elgin "rescued" the Elgin Marbles from Athens in 1803 and they were exhibited in London the reaction was

complete adoration. All things Greek were definitely "in" from sculpture to garden ornaments, from ladies' gowns to ladies' Greek hair styles. Thus it was that the buildings of Cheltenham were greatly influenced by the elegance of past civilisations.

During the first half of the 18th century the spa towns, Leamington, Bath, Buxton, Tunbridge and others, were to a great extent competing with each other for this very lucrative market. Not content with simply selling their water, they were creating a socially acceptable environment in which the visitor came as much to be seen as to

*The Pittville Pump Room in its beautiful parkland setting, on the outskirts of Cheltenham*

take the waters. The developers constructed promenades, band stands, billiard rooms, gardens, theatres, ball rooms, restaurants, rows of smart shops, concert halls, tea rooms and all other niceties with which they could persuade the visitors to part with their money. Whole families came for weeks on end living in furnished accommodation or 'lodgings' and when not taking the waters there were many other social diversions to become involved in; not least of all at Cheltenham was the race course with its famous Gold Cup which was first run in 1819.

Unfortunately like all good things, fashions change and the completion of the Pittville Pump Room heralded the beginning of that change for Cheltenham. The upper and middle classes of Regency England were going through a period of change and there was opposition to the lifestyles of the very rich, not least of all from the church. The Evangelist Francis Close set about the town's aristocracy with a vengeance, chiding them for their flippant lifestyle and loose love life: he even tried to abolish the race course. In this he was not successful but he did oppose the building of a rail link to the town when many other towns were developing a transport network which gave them a rail link to the nation's capital. As a result of his opposition Cheltenham had to wait until 1847 for this task to be completed. But the change of attitude was not entirely to do with the church in spite of a renewed interest in religion: the seaside holiday with its fresh, new image was making inroads into the waters of the spa towns' businesses.

As the spa trade declined new residents came to Cheltenham, many of them being ex-empire builders, tea planters, civil servants, army officers and the like. The town had much to offer their discerning requirements, for here there were large houses with large gardens to be had at reasonable prices and there was a plentiful supply of domestic servants. There were clubs, restaurants, good shops and schools for the offspring and there was very adequate hunting and shooting to be had in the surrounding Cotswold countryside. Today Cheltenham is still very much a residential town, with light industry and the administrative centres of the Universities Central Council, the Countryside Commission and, perhaps best known, the Government Communications Centre, G.C.H.Q.

**CHELTENHAM**

P  Parking
T  Toilets
1  St. Mary's Church
2  Museum
3  Coach Station
4  Cheltenham's Ladies College
5  The Queen's Hotel
6  Town Hall
7  Regency Terrace and the Neptune Fountain

# 7: Chipping Campden

Of Chipping Campden, John Masefield wrote:

On Campden wold the skylark sings,
In Campden town the traveller finds
The inward peace that beauty brings
To bless and heal tormented minds.

Whether it is the most beautiful town in the Cotswolds, as has been suggested by some writers, is a matter of debate but it is certainly a handsome one. Its buildings are, in the main all fronting directly on to the main street and unlike Broadway or Moreton-in-Marsh there are very few grass verges between the roadway and the build-ings, which are for the good part, three storeys high. Its main street has a slight curve to it as it accommodates a collection of old inns, shops and fine houses some of which have an upper storey of timber frame but in the main the buildings are of fine Cotswold stone. Occasionally this fine thoroughfare is broken by a side alley, an old archway or side street but otherwise it consists of a continuous line of flat fronted or angle bowed buildings all blending well one with another.

I have often felt, and I am sure I'm not alone, that the most tragic event that befell Chipping Campden was the burning to the ground in 1645 of what must have been one of the most magnificent houses of its time in all of England. Campden House was built, as far as we understand, in the Italian style with much ornamental detail to pavilions which flanked a wide terrace. Sir Henry Bard and his troops were garrisoned at the house whilst the owner was fighting elsewhere for the Royalist cause and when the army required re-enforcing for the battle of Naseby the house was put to the torch in case it should fall into enemy hands. Ironically the Cromwellians did not approach any closer than Warwick! The ruins of Campden House, to the right of the church, are fairly extensive. Some of the south front and two pavilions at the end of the terrace with two unusual gazebos are each side of the main entrance. All serve to show the outstanding grandeur of what was enclosed by the outer walls. Alas, there is little else that stands today, except for the former stables that are opposite the almshouses and known as the Court House.

This is the town, or a small part of that, which the visitor sees and enthuses over today, but the development of Campden commenced a long time before the Civil War, in fact back in the times of the Saxons. The very name of Campden is derived from Saxon words *Camp* which possibly meant

*St James' Church beyond the 17th century Almshouses*

*The Market Hall*

'battle' and *Dere* meaning 'Valley in the woodland'. Camp refers to the great battle fought here around AD670 between Ina, the King of the West Saxons and the marauders from the west, the Welsh. They were in fact the remains of the ancient Britons who had gone west after the Roman dispersal and the Saxons moved in from the east. This, as far as can be proved, was the last great battle in our island between Saxon and Ancient Britain.

Later, we know not how much later, the distinctive title of 'Ceapon' or 'Cheapon' appears. In the Saxon language it meant 'barter' or 'to buy', 'to purchase' or 'trade for', thus as at Chipping Norton in Oxfordshire, we have here Chipping Campden, a place where trading is carried out.

The first real recognition of trading came during Henry II's time for he granted the first charter to the town in 1185 enabling it to market wool and other goods that were the produce of the surrounding weald, hence the town developed as a market place.

At the time of Domesday, Campden was called the 'Hundred of Kiftsgate' which may have meant 'along a ridge'. A tablet at the old Norman Chapel at nearby Broad Campden shows that the Manorial Rights belonged to King Harold before the Nor-

man Conquest. The Earl of Chester, a nephew of King William, then acquired the rights; later they passed to Hugh de Gondeville who was one of the assassins of Thomas a Becket. The buttresses, well worn with age, which are built into the Town Hall are thought to be part of a much earlier building which stood on the same site around 1180. It is assumed that as the Lord of Campden at the time was Hugh de Gondeville, he built a chapel dedicated to Catherine of Alexandria to help clear his conscience and it is these buttresses that still stand today.

It may be difficult for today's visitor to appreciate, but it is quite probable that during its heyday Chipping Campden was the busiest of all the wool trading towns. During medieval times there were other parts of the country that developed and prospered from the sale and trade of wool but the Cotswolds was certainly the most important in all of England. Chipping Campden, it seems, was the 'capital'.

Throughout the whole of the Cotswolds there were numerous rich wool merchants and each town seems to have had its own

*The elaborate gateway to the former mansion of Sir Baptist Hicks*

group of individual, rich and influential families. One such family in Chipping Campden was the Grevel's. In fact William Grevel became known as the 'Flower of the wool merchants of England'. Grevel's House, built in 1390, stands near the end of the High Street and has been changed little since then. It must have been one of the few stone buildings in the town in those days and even today, surrounded by such fine stone buildings, it stands out with its quite distinctive, two storey bay windows as being very much influenced by Flemish architecture.

Just opposite is the Woolstaplers Hall constructed about 1340 by the Cotterills. It was in the heavily timbered upper room of this fine building that Grevel and other woolstaplers carried out the business of selling wool.

Further down the street is the Old Grammar School which was founded and endowed by John Fereby; an inscription reads 'Schola Grammaticae 1487'. It was rebuilt in 1628 after Sir Baptist Hicks another great benefactor of Campden, brought a court action against the trustees and re-endowed it himself. The building is of three storeys with four small and one large gable.

The town's Market Hall was built in 1627, also by Sir Baptist Hicks. He was a very rich London banker, a colleague of Shakespeare and a friend of James I. The lovely old Market Hall is a fine centrepiece for the town. It is gabled with open bays and was designed for the sale of domestic goods. The windows on the upper floor were enclosed in order to comply with the requirements of window tax.

If Sir Baptist Hicks lost his own house as a result of the Civil War his fine Almshouses still stand close to the entrance to his former home. They were built in the shape of a capital I which at that time was read as a 'J' as a mark of honour to James I.

Designed to accommodate twelve persons they are a fine example of the Cotswold stonemason's craft, having well fitting stonework and high pointed roofs with pinnacles at the corners.

The Church of St. James occupies a site of an earlier church at Campden. Today's church is almost entirely 15th century, with 'updating' by the Victorians thankfully kept to a minimum. The entrance to the south porch is through an avenue of lime trees planted in 1770, the twelve trees representing the twelve apostles. The porch itself has been modified since it was built in the 14th century and has a niche over the doorway which originally contained a figure of Our Lady. Before the Reformation the church was dedicated to Our Lady, after which the dedication was to St. James.

The South Chapel contains memorials to the benevolent families of the town - Sir Baptist Hicks of course, and the Noel families. The effigies of Sir Baptist and Lady Elizabeth are thought to be by Nicholas Stone. On the South Wall Sir Edward Noel is depicted. He was the son-in-law of Sir Baptist and was killed at Oxford in 1642, a victim of the Civil War. The monument to his daughter by Francesco Fanelli represents a most tragic happening, for she died of blood poisoning after pricking her finger while working with coloured silks. The

*Two storey bay windows at the Grevel House*

49

pulpit is Jacobean and was a gift from Sir Baptist Hicks in 1612. The church contains many other memorials and brasses but for me its fine stone structure is of great interest.

The tower of St. James's church dominates the town, rising as it does from slightly higher ground at the northeastern edge of the town. The tower measures 120ft high and while having considerable detail it is not too fussy but is well proportioned with graceful corner buttresses and is considered to be amongst the finest in the Cotswolds. The nave at about half the height of the tower was probably built by

*The church of St James*

the same master mason who built the nave at Northleach. William Grevel is always attributed with generous donations to the church and in his Will of 1401 he did bequeath a legacy for the very purpose of developing further this fine building. There were other rich wool merchants who gave with generosity but certainly William Grevel set a good example, enabling much work to be carried out on the church from around 1390 to 1402. The memorial brass to this chief benefactor is said to be the largest in Gloucestershire; at over 8ft x 4ft, it depicts Grevel the merchant with his first wife Marian. Surmounted by a canopy it includes his merchant's mark and his coat of arms. In the southwest corner of the church a set of steps leads to a small 14th century room above the porch. This is the Muniment Room, formerly a school room, which now houses the church valuables and documents. These are watched over by a Norman corbel of a bear with a muzzle which is the only survivor of the original Norman church.

During the 18th and 19th centuries when other towns were developing their milling potential with the aid of water power, Chipping Campden declined in importance as no suitable water source was at hand. However, during the early 1900s, C.R. Ashbee, a disciple of William Morris and a follower of Ruskin, came to the town with his Guild of Handicrafts. Since then arts and crafts have thrived here and the Campden Trust, formed in 1929, has done much to preserve and restore the local architecture.

While each writer on Chipping Campden will relate to the unique tale of the 'Campden Wanderer', I wonder to myself just how unique this tale really is. With tongue in cheek I will therefore put pen to paper to simplify as best I am able the tale of the 'Chipping Wonder'.

It seems that on the 16th August 1660, William Harrison, who was the steward to

Lady Campden, was sent out to collect rents of the properties that she owned. William Harrison was then about 70 years of age and she being a lady did not give her age away. William did not return from this simple local mission and although his wife sent out John Perry, a servant, he could not be found and as Perry was furthering his enquiries in the direction of Charringworth he met William Reed and informed him of his task. Later he passed John Pierce but it was not until the next day that he reached Charringworth and made enquiries about Mr. Harrison at the homes of William Curtis and Edward Plaisterer. Later John

*Berrington Mill*

Perry stated that Mr. Harrison had been murdered by his brother Richard Perry and that the body had been thrown into the water near Berrington Mill. Richard and John Perry together with their mother were later charged with the murder of William Harrison and appeared at the assize at Gloucester where the Judge, Sir Christopher Turner refused to try them because the body was still missing. At the next assize all three were tried by Judge Sir Robert Hyde and in spite of their protest all were found to be guilty; they were executed on Broadway Hill. Two years later up turned William Harrison with a tale of being kidnapped while collecting the rents and being taken as a galley slave by Algerian pirates. He said he had eventually escaped and returned to England via Portugal. It certainly sounds a most unlikely tale but unfortunately nothing it seems was proved or clarified - but in his absence three innocent people had wrongly been executed.

Bought by the National Trust in 1928, Dovers Hill is a favourite area, when winter is over, with local kite flying enthusiasts. Due to its high, unsheltered position it is also a fine vantage point and affords an excellent panorama across the Vale of Evesham below. Its name is derived from Robert Dover who was a successful lawyer during the 1600s and was the founder of the Cotswold Games which are held in the surrounding area. In those early days the games were much more rough and tumble than present day sporting events and consisted of such contests as wrestling, horse racing, stick fighting, bear baiting, cock fighting and perhaps the most unusual sport of shin-kicking. The games, even mentioned by Shakespeare, were so well known in their day that it is said that King

*Window shopping at Chipping Campden*

*The Martins and Little Martins*

51

James gave his approval by presenting Robert Dover with a suit and feathered hat to wear when pronouncing the games 'open'. In 1852 when the supporters were frequently becoming drunk and out of hand, the games were disbanded. As recently as 1951 the games were revived in a much modified form for the Festival of Britain and are now held around the last Friday in May. They are followed the day after by the Scuttlebrook Wake, the festival at Chipping Campden.

The visitor to Chipping Campden would be well advised not to miss the Manor of Hidcote just a few miles to the north of the town. Now famous for its gardens and owned by the National Trust, the house dates from the 17th century and was bought in 1907 by the American, Lawrence Johnston who developed this horticultural masterpiece. Close by are the gardens of Kiftsgate House and about half a mile distant is the fine 16th century Hidcote House.

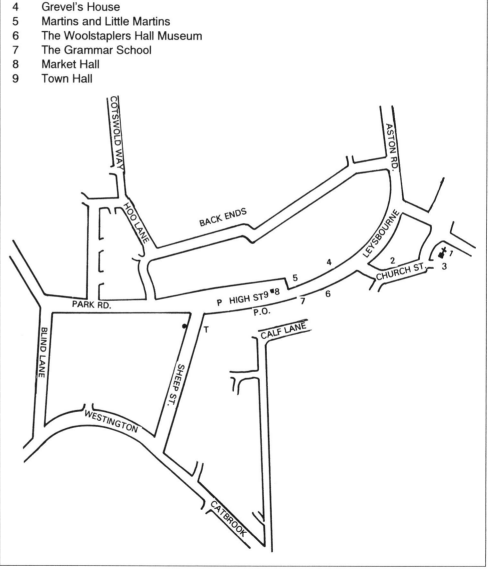

**CHIPPING CAMPDEN**

| | |
|---|---|
| P | Parking |
| P.O. | Post Office |
| T | Toilets |
| 1 | Church of St. James |
| 2 | Almshouses in Church Street |
| 3 | Site of Campden House |
| 4 | Grevel's House |
| 5 | Martins and Little Martins |
| 6 | The Woolstaplers Hall Museum |
| 7 | The Grammar School |
| 8 | Market Hall |
| 9 | Town Hall |

# 8: Chipping Norton

Chipping Norton is the highest town in Oxfordshire at around 650ft above sea level. It has an attractive High Street which joins the Market Square where, in times gone by, horse fairs and markets where held. Around the town centre there still remain shops and inns whose foundations were laid down at various times during the last 300 years but most of the town's architecture dates from a more recent period when the town was well known for milling. The Guildhall at one end of the market place dates from the 16th century. At the opposite end the Town Hall is modern by comparison being a solid, neo-classical building of 1842. It was designed by G.S. Repton who worked for a time with John Nash and with his own father Humphrey Repton. There is much evidence around the town centre of the town's prosperity during the 18th century when a number of the earlier buildings were given a false front in order to project a more modern, up-market and fashionable façade. In the High Street The White Hart Hotel and The Bunch of Grapes in Middle Row are both good examples of this practice.

The development of the town can be traced back to a much earlier time and it is thought that the ancient British tribe, the Dobunni, may well have settled in the area close to present day Chipping Norton. It is possible also that they made pilgrimages to the local stone circle which we know today as the Rollright Stones. But this is ancient history; a little more recently the Romans seem to have found this area an agreeable place to stay, their legions departing shortly after AD400. Roman currency, pottery, bronze brooches and a carved stone head are amongst the items found in and around the town. The carved head appears to be that of a man with a good head of curly hair and a handsome beard. A cast of the head is in the Ashmolean Museum at Oxford.

Later again, during the 10th century, Saxons and Danes battled at nearby Hook Norton and at Sarsden in 1016 the fighting resulted in Edmund Ironside defeating King Canute. In spite of all the trouble, however, historians seem certain that some kind of community had become established here prior to the 11th century and that the town's name was derived from the Anglo Saxon *chepying* and in later times *chipping*, but until the 13th century it was simply called Norton.

At the time of Domesday the town was held as part of the Earldom of Swein, son of Earl Godwin and brother of Harold, the last of the Saxon Kings. Aluric Welp and

*High Street, Chipping Norton*

Ulward White were then the Lords of the Manor which included present day Chipping Norton and Over Norton, the community at that time consisting of about fifty families.

Some time during the 12th century a 'castle', probably a wooden structure, was built. Alas, all that remains today are the foundations known as the Castle Mounds. Its vulnerable position in the valley near today's church would indicate that it could have been constructed not for defence but for pleasure. Wychwood Forest was close by and hunting was greatly enjoyed by the wealthy. Historians are fairly certain that

*Chipping Norton, High Street looking towards Horsefair*

the 'castle' had passed its peak well before the Middle Ages were over.

Whilst there is no documentary evidence to confirm or deny that a monastery ever existed at Chipping Norton it was recorded in 1801 that some such remains were still visible. Until about a hundred years ago an archway was still to be seen as part of the wall in one of the houses in Guildhall Place. In the High Street, below No. 20, a vaulted ceiling, similar to that of a church porch, may have been part of a former monastic chapel. This chapel may, however, have belonged to the Guild of the Holy Trinity, since evidence points to certain properties in the High Street having belonged to the Guild.

If, however, there was never a monastery at Chipping Norton itself, it could have been that there was no need for one as only a mile or so away there was a priory at Cold Norton. This was founded during the late 1100s and had a hospital which cared for the old and the sick of the area. It was not a wealthy priory and partially due to the demands made upon its hospitality and partly due to bad management by its Priors, the establishment continually experienced financial problems. When the last Prior, John Wootton, died in 1496 there was no one to take his place and a few years into the next century the Priory, together with its lands and manor, were passed to the King.

The early history of the town's Church of St. Mary is quite vague but by the reign of Henry II it is clear that the church of 'Noton' was 'owned' by the Abbey of St. Peter's at Gloucester. Some time after 1170 it became the church of St. Thomas a Becket but a century or two later its dedication was again changed to its present one, St. Mary the Virgin. There seems to be some confusion regarding just what the church consisted of before the 14th century. Evidence shows that by this time it was enlarged and the north and south aisles had by then been

added: the windows in the north aisles incidentally date from a century later. The east window in the south aisle is thought to have been transferred from nearby Bruerne Abbey in 1535. In spite of the Victorians' enthusiasium for restoration, much of today's church dates from the 14th and 15th centuries when, like other Cotswold towns, the prosperity of the wool trade was reflected in beautiful houses, grand estates and fine churches. It is quite likely that John de Gadesdon wrote his *Rosa Anglica* while he was rector at Chipping Norton. He was instituted in 1321 and became well known throughout his lifetime as a respected

*Stone carved second century Roman head*

physician and an author of medical information, so much so that over a quarter of a century later his written information was still being studied in parts of Europe. As recognition of his work for medicine he was elevated to the position of Doctor of Medicine and King's Clerk in 1332 and fourteen years later he was presented with a gold rose by the Prince of Wales.

The building of the church's nave is ascribed to John Ashefylde and a brass effigy of his wife is on the wall of the north aisle. Over on the west wall of the nave the remains of a Norman or early English Transitional arch can clearly be seen and the Chancel, divided from the nave by a rood screen, is little altered since the 14th century.

Chipping Norton certainly has a fine and lofty church but for me one of its most interesting features is its entrance porch. Legend has it that the porch was built to commemorate a very special event in the history of the church. During the year 1302 there were five devils who were cast out of the church by the priest, Henry of Winchcombe. It was said that the devils were chased by Henry through the market place where he lost them amongst a flock of sheep and it was this 'casting out' of the devils that warranted the building of this unique hexagonal piece of church architecture. There are only two other examples of hexagonal church porches in England: one is to the southwest at St. Mary Redcliffe, Bristol, and the other is to the northwest at St. Lawrence, Ludlow. Here at Chipping Norton on either side of the porch's interior is a stone seat with a lancet window above it and at the intersections of the groined roof, grinning devils look down on those who

Left:        The Church of St Mary the Virgin
Right:       A grinning Devil inside the porch of
             the Church of St Mary the Virgin
Below right: The hexagonal porch at St Mary the
             Virgin

enter. The doorway into the church is 14th century and close by a flight of stone steps leads up to the priest's room above this most unusual porch.

Possibly the most bizarre happening regarding the church at Chipping Norton is the hanging from the tower of the vicar, Henry Joyce, in 1549. He led a revolt against the replacement of the Latin Mass by the English prayer book of Archbishop Cramner. The revolt led to a riot and as he was the ring leader he was made to pay with his life.

Just out of the church and into Church Street stands one of the most picturesque rows of cottages in Oxfordshire. Originally they formed eight dwellings and were, as the gable inscription reads, "The work and gift of Henry Cornish, gent 1640." In his Will he declared that the cottages should be for ever used as Almshouses. They were to house eight poor widows who resided in the town for seven years and who must be of honest and godly life and conversation. In addition to these he purchased a further twelve dwellings within the town and left them to his great nephew and his heirs to be used for similar charitable purposes. Thus Henry Cornish whilst being a very rich man was also a very charitable one.

A little closer to the church just across the road and above the garage doorway is a simple memorial to eight R.A.F. aircrew who died in a night flying accident on 21st August 1942. A timely reminder of the region's connection with the R.A.F. during the Second World War.

Perhaps the opposite number to the charitable Henry Cornish was James Hind who, in his day, was as notorious in these parts as Dick Turpin. He was born in Chipping Norton in 1616, the son of a

*Above: Contrasting architectural styles at Chipping Norton, The Blue Boar*

*Left: The Almshouses*

saddler, and on leaving school became an apprentice butcher. He soon turned his back on the meat trade however and travelled to London to join up with Thomas Allen, another highwayman of the day. During the Civil War Hind rode with a horse troop of Sir William Compton but after the Royalist defeat at Naseby he returned to his old 'trade' of highwayman before rejoining Charles II at the Battle of Worcester. Escaping after the battle he made for London but was captured and condemned for high treason in 1652. He was hung, drawn and

*The Bliss Mill, Chipping Norton*

quartered and as was the justice in those days, his head was set on a pike at Bridge Gate, Worcester. He was not one of Chipping Norton's most successful sons.

As for most of England and for the Cotswolds in particular the days of the English Civil War were dark indeed and Chipping Norton was aware of both sides of the troubles. Horse dragoons of the rebels were in 1640 reputedly plundering the local villages and on the 15th March of that year the King gave orders that two regiments of horse were to be sent to the town to save the situation. By 6th June the King had left Oxford and was at Burford with a large

army of foot and horse troops while Cromwell himself was at Chipping Norton. Whilst there are no records of battles in the town, there was much bloodshed at the time at nearby Stow-on-the-Wold.

During the mid 1700s the production of cloth played a most important part in the town's economy. Working from premises in New Street in 1746, William Fowler employed local woolcombers, spinners and weavers and successfully developed a local manufacturing business. But nine years later the son of a clothier, one Thomas Bliss, came to town and in 1758 married Ann Insall whose father gave them part of

William Fowler's cloth business as a wedding present. In due course a son was born to the Bliss's and it was he, William Bliss, who took over the business in 1790, later moving to an old flour mill on the Common and developing it into a factory with a reputation for Chipping Norton tweed.

Eighty years later and managed by the next generation of Bliss's, the mill employed 700 people and had an annual turnover of over a quarter of a million pounds, a very considerable amount of money at that time. By 1851, the Upper Mill was enlarged and

*Distons Lane*

*The Town Hall*

57

steam machinery installed. The Lower Mill was completely rebuilt and enlarged by 1865, when all manner of cloth from railway rugs to army clothing was being produced. In 1872 a boiler exploded killing three men and destroying the mill but in less than a year the Bliss Valley Mill was rebuilt. With its large domed tower it was intended by its designer, the Lancashire mill architect George Woodhouse, that it should look like a large country house and in this aim he was certainly successful. However the heyday for the Bliss's and for the town's prosperity were fast drawing to a conclusion. Foreign competition meant a general decline in British manufactured cloth. The Bliss's fortunes dwindled until just before the turn of the century the family left the town and the mill was taken over by the Birmingham Banking Company. George Woodhouse's handsome creation still dominates the approach to the town from the west and was converted into flats in 1980.

The visitor to the town will find the small Theatre in Spring Street quite unusual, formerly it was a Salvation Army Citadel. In the past its inception as a citadel was not so peacefully accepted as the stone set into the auditorium wall pronounces: "These stones were laid by one hundred of those who through great persecution boldly and conscientiously serve their God." Used as a furniture store for a time, the building was purchased during the early 1970s enabling the theatre to open in 1975. The theatre is at present being updated and it is hoped that this will enable it to progress to more ambitious programmes. I wish it well for the future!

Just a few miles to the north of the town are the ancient Rollright Stones, as important some say as Stonehenge itself, though

*The Guild Hall*

*The Whispering Knights*

nowhere near as impressive in size. They should not be missed by the visitor to Chipping Norton. The Rollright Stones is a prehistoric stone circle set on a 700ft ridge and informed opinion puts its age at about 3,500 years. The King's Men consist of about seventy pitted, weather beaten uprights set in a circle of about 100ft diameter. Further across the field five upright stones, known as the Whispering Knights, are thought to indicate a burial chamber. Across the road stands the strangely shaped 8ft high King Stone, apparently watching over the slope towards the village of Long Compton. It is interesting to note that Sir Arthur Evans,

well known for his work at the ancient site of Knosses on the Greek island of Crete, visited the Rollright Stones in 1890. He was so fascinated by them that he produced a paper about the folk stories associated with them. Over the centuries many legends have grown up around these stones, one of which has it that in days gone by a certain King was intent on conquering England and he met a witch. The witch turned the King and his men to stone, then she did likewise to his knights who were whispering together, thus the stones have names and positions of status, from King to knight to men!

*The King Stone*

## CHIPPING NORTON

| | |
|---|---|
| P | Parking |
| P.O. | Post Office |
| T | Toilets |
| 1 | Church of St. Mary |
| 2 | Castle Mounds |
| 3 | Almshouses |
| 4 | Theatre |
| 5 | Old Guild Hall |
| 6 | Town Hall |

# 9: Cirencester

*The magnificent south porch of Cirencester Parish Church*

Soon after the year AD43 the Emperor to be, Vespasion, was pushing westward with his Roman army following their recent invasion of Britain and a few years later they were to construct the famous Fosse Way in order to link together Lincoln in the east with Exeter in Devon. It just happened that at Cirencester it was decided to build one of a series of forts along the route from which the Romans patrolled the new highway and the adjacent lands. Within 30 years the Romans had moved their front line further north in England and west to Wales; it was then that a major settlement was developed for the British tribe, the Dobunni. It was close to the River Churn and just a few miles north of today's city. Excavations here have revealed many pre-Roman artifacts, coins and the Mints at which they were made.

The Roman development at Cirencester was named Corinium Dorbunnorum. Covering some 240 acres, it was at the time second only in size to Londinium. The old city defences are still visible in the form of an earth bank beside the river in the grounds of the Abbey and along Beeches Road. The ramparts were made by heaping up earth then facing it with stone; over the centuries the latter was seen as a valuable building material. The Roman town probably had four gates with roads that intersected at the city's centre somewhere near the crossing from Tower Street to Southgate, close to Lewis Lane. Evidence shows that the Romans had a Forum, a large Basilica, a market place enclosed by purpose built shops and numerous religious shrines within their city. It is evident that later on, during the 4th century, Corinium became the capital of the region known as Britannia Prima and it probably had all the amenities of any other important city within the Roman Empire.

With the demise of this empire Cirencester was taken by Ceawlin of Wessex following his defeat of the British Kings at Dyrham in AD577. It was probably these Saxons, building their new places of residence to the northern edge of the former Roman city, who put to good use much of the ready cut stonework of the Roman ramparts.

William Fitz-Osbern seems to have inherited Cirencester soon after the Norman Conquest and soon built a castle on the Fosse Way at the southwestern town entrance. This stood until some time in the Middle Ages.

During the early 1100s the old Saxon church was developed as a monastic Abbey with the King as patron. As he also happened to be the Lord of the Manor he provided a new church for the townsfolk. This resulted in Cirencester having the Church of St. John, which is still very much in existence, in addition to the Augustine Abbey of St. Mary which unfortunately only lasted in its entirety for a mere 400 years or so. At the Dissolution of the Monasteries it was, along with many others, pulled down on the orders of Henry VIII. The site was then sold and anything of value was confiscated.

The Abbey of St. Mary's had been consecrated in 1176 during the reign of Henry II but today the only building remaining is the Norman Gatehouse which stands as something of a monument to what must have been a magnificent piece of architecture before 1539. Today a plaque indicates the site of the Abbey.

Just as other Cotswold towns had prospered during the Middle Ages from the numerous stages in the production, weaving, selling and dealing in wool and its associated trades, so too did Cirencester. The Weavers Guild can in fact be traced back to 1580 when all those tradespeople connected with wool pressed hard for the King's Court of the Exchequer to recognise a charter for their merchant guild. After their failure to do so they were given the right in 1571 to have two persons freely elected to serve their interests in Parliament.

At that time, as at other periods throughout history, those with wealth built fine houses, large estates, lived the good life and gave to the church. So it was here at Cirencester, as a result of which the parish church is one which was built largely on the profits from the wool trade and is frequently referred to as one of the Cotswolds 'wool' churches.

For the visitor the very striking lines of the large Church of St. John makes it difficult to appreciate that all this fine architecture started out as an ordinary parish church set beside the gateway of the enormously wealthy and influential Abbey of St. Mary's. Over the years and as the town developed, the market place has been established right outside the church and the houses and the shops of the town have closed in around it, consequently the unusual three storey porch now opens into this busy part of the town centre. The porch, said to be unique, was added to the church in 1500 when the extra rooms above the entrance were required as office chambers to be used by the Town and the Abbot. It is undoubtedly a fine piece of building on its own, being Perpendicular in style, with a decorated parapet at the same height as the roof of the nave, and it is finished with pinnacles. Inside the porch's stone roof is carved into a stout fan tracery.

Inside the church the vastness of the space, both of height and width of the nave, are most apparent. During the early part of the 16th century the earlier nave was modified and heightened thereby creating the spaciousness.

A window having seven lights is above the chancel arch and this is a feature which, in the main, is found only in Cotswold 'wool' churches. Within the numerous side chapels people who made contributions to the church are remembered with memorials, plaques, tombs and brasses. As the visitor moves round the church its history becomes apparent from the time of the Norman building replacing the earlier Anglo-Saxon church. On the south arch of the chancel the base part of the short broad pillar is of Roman origin and was no doubt incorporated into this fine structure by its medieval stonemasons. The church's 15th century pulpit takes the form of a wine glass. It is carved in open stone tracery and decorated in green and red.

*The Norman gatehouse. All that remains of Cirencester Abbey*

*One of Cirencester's ancient doorways*

Above the west end of the church stands the quite graceful tower, two flying buttresses being incorporated into its design as it was built skyward in order to support its lean lines. In the tower the ringing chamber houses possibly the oldest peal of bells in the world. They are certainly the oldest in England.

During the Civil War the townsfolk of Cirencester were strong supporters of Cromwell but the large estate owners understandably sided with the King. In 1643 the town was taken by Prince Rupert and the King followed this by a visit to the Abbey House. The town was later recaptured by the Parliamentarians. Following the King's defeat at Worcester in 1651 his son, who later became Charles II, passed through Cirencester beneath a heavy disguise whilst making good his escape to the coast. It is claimed that he stayed the night at both The Royal Oak and The Crown Inn while another claim is that he stayed at The Sun, or was it The Fleece? When he return to Cirencester as King of England in 1663 he stayed with Sir Henry Poole from whom Cirencester Park was purchased by the Bathurst family.

Less than a hundred years later John Wesley had preached in the town on a number of occasions and a Methodist church was founded. The Powells provided funds for schools, at one of which one of England's most famous sons, Edward Jenner, the discoverer of smallpox vaccine, whose memorial is in Gloucester Cathedral, was educated. You can see Rebecca Powell's School in Gloucester Street.

By the late 1700s England had been seized by 'Canal mania'. Canals were being constructed all over the land. At Cirencester in 1789 an arm of the Thames and Severn Canal was opened and it was from this period that Welsh slate became available for the roofs of the town's buildings. Similarly

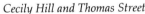
*Cecily Hill and Thomas Street*

coal had only been available in small quantities but with the development of these new inland waterways the town had a plentiful supply of fuel from Staffordshire in the north and the Forest of Dean in the south.

As with the commercial life of all the country's canals they were soon to be eclipsed by the development of the steam locomotive and by 1841 the town had a railway station on the branch line from Kemble which formed part of the Great Western network. By 1883 the Midland and South Western Junction Railway linked the town to Swindon by way of Watermoor. Eight years later it was linked to Cheltenham via Andoversford. Unfortunately the railway transport systems suffered as did many others in the 1960s.

The visitor will no doubt be aware of the Bathhurst's residence at Cirencester Park. The house which stands behind a 40ft yew hedge planted in 1720, is not open to the public but the huge parkland is available for all to enjoy. To visit it go from Park Street into Cecily Hill which was the old road to Stroud. The houses on the hill date from the late 1600s to the early 20th century with various dates carved on different properties and no one could miss the Barracks on the right. Dating from 1857 the Barracks is modern by Cotswold standards but this imposing example of Victorian architecture was built to accommodate the Royal North Gloucestershire Militia. Just beyond are the decorative gates leading to the five mile long Broadwalk of Cirencester Park.

Cirencester's heart is its curving Market Place. Once it was packed with tiny shops trading in all manner of things. Alleys and narrow lanes ran between with names such as Butter Row, Shoe Lane and Butchers Row. In the mid 1300s they were complained about and the Abbot was informed of their gradual encroachment

and eventually they were removed. Today the market place has a bright and pleasant appearance and so it should as it contains so much pleasant architecture which enhances the already mentioned church and porch.

The Fleece Hotel has a much restored timber front while many of the other buildings appear to be Georgian or Stuart but behind their façades some are timber framed Tudor in origin. The Corn Hall dates from 1862. It is constructed of Cotswold stone and has fine carvings by H.C. Frith above the windows, while the Dunstall Hall at 27 Park Street is a most

*Rebecca Powell's school in Gloucester Street*

*The Battery, Cecily Hill*

interesting house of the 17th century.

Throughout my travels in the Cotswolds I have come across a number of old lock-ups; frequently they have had a dome shaped roof. At Cirencester in 1837 the little building known as the Dumpling House was moved stone by stone to its present site. Here it became part of the workhouse, newly built and ready to receive its new residents at that time. During more recent times the old buildings have been refurbished and used as council offices. Now the Cirencester museums service has installed a sequence of displays showing the history of 'lock-ups' within the county of Gloucester.

*The Fleece Hotel*

**CIRENCESTER**

| | |
|---|---|
| P | Parking |
| T | Toilets |
| 1 | Church of St. John the Baptist |
| 2 | The Fleece Hotel |
| 3 | The Norman Gatehouse to the Abbey |
| 4 | Rebecca Powell's School |
| 5 | The Barracks |
| 6 | The Yew Hedge |
| 7 | Museum |

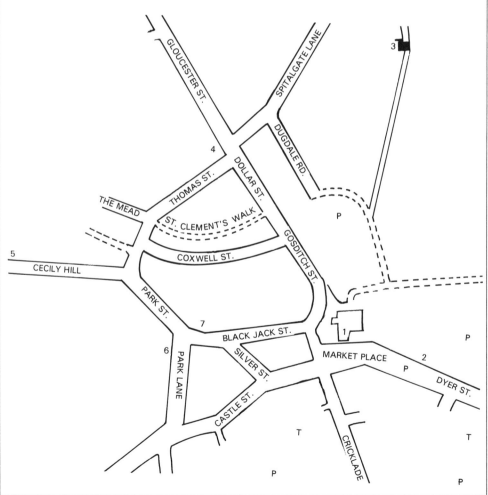

# 10: Gloucester

*A delicate filagree in stone, Gloucester Cathedral*

Charles Dickens is said to have declared that Gloucester was a wonderful and misleading city. Then, as now, Gloucester was a city with a rich history which has resulted in many fine examples of architecture from different periods with one of England's outstanding cathedrals at its centre.

The contribution made at Gloucester to the history of England is quite unique. Not only was Gloucester the place where the Domesday Book was commissioned, it was also where Henry III was crowned and where Edward II was buried after his murder at Berkeley Castle. However to generations of children it is where there lived a tailor and the city is the setting in which the magic spun around him really happened. The story was by Beatrix Potter and her book was *The Tailor of Gloucester*.

It seems that she was a frequent visitor to her cousin Caroline Hutton, who resided at the Grange at nearby Harescombe, and it was while on one of these visits that she heard the story of the tailor. For those who do not know the story, the tailor was John Prichard who was working on a suit for the City's mayor to wear to his first ceremonial engagement. With some work still to complete on the suit, the tailor hastened home for the weekend only to find on his

return the following Monday that the job was done except for one buttonhole. A note attached to the waistcoat read "No More Twist". The pleasantly surprised tailor was said to have put the waistcoat in the shop window with a note pointing out that his waistcoats were made at night by the fairies, which was of course great publicity. Having no doubt smiled at this Victorian publicity stunt it obviously dawned on Beatrix Potter that there might be the basis of a story in it and with a little modification, the tailor becoming very poor with threadbare clothing and the fairies being changed into mice, she had hit upon a best selling children's formula. (The Beatrix Potter Shop is in College Court.) This, when compared to Gloucester's past is quite modern history but what happened during the days before Charles Dickens and Beatrix Potter?

Gloucester was in ancient times the lowest point at which the River Severn could be forded and it was probably for this reason that the Romans, eager to push on to Wales, found it to be as favourable a place as any of the others they had come across in the Cotswolds, from which to press on with their conquest of Britain. Occupation of the land had been fairly straightforward. The natives, the Dobunni, were in the main happy to carry on farming the land and as

*Beatrix Potter shop, Gloucester*

in other nearby areas of occupation the Romans set up a camp at Kingsholm. A timber fortress was constructed about AD45 but it was taken down after about fifteen years when a new one was built on a higher vantage point having good visibility across the river at Gloucester. To some extent this early Roman military settlement influenced the layout of the old centre of Gloucester for generations to come. Northgate, Southgate, Eastgate and Westgate streets, together with other thoroughfares enclosed by them, all roughly follow a similar pattern to those laid out so many years before.

When their armies moved westwards into Wales the camp at Gloucester became a colonial town and as had happened at Colchester and Lincoln in earlier years, the former fortress of Gloucester was converted into a Roman city. It had houses, shops and market areas, in fact all the facilities that a civilised society would require. It became home to the new colonists, retired Roman soldiers who then became the nucleus of the inhabitants of the new town. This colony, known as Glevum, developed, multiplied and prospered until well into the 4th century but when the Saxons invaded Britain in 409 there were few Roman troops left to oppose them, the British garrisons having been reduced on many occasions to take part in the fighting in other parts of the Empire. As with numerous towns and cities throughout the land the contribution made by the Romans to the founding of Gloucester was enormous.

By the late 6th century Gloucester, together with Bath and Cirencester, had been occupied by the Anglo-Saxons and by 679, Osric, King of the Hwicce, founded a Monastery which he dedicated to St. Peter. The monastery was led by his sister Kyneburgh and it had provision for both male and female inmates.

Before the end of the 9th century the invading Danes were close to Gloucester

and like other places in west Mercia the town was well defended against the raiding heathens; the supervision of this work being carried out by Alfred the Great's daughter, Aethelflaed. It is interesting to note that it was also she who founded, just a little to the north of the ancient church of St. Mary de Lode, the minster church of St. Oswald in about AD900. The ruins visible today indicate that the building had additions and modifications carried out right up until the 16th century. Much of the original stonework was material reused from the earlier Roman city. It would have had few windows and its richly carved and brightly painted interior would have relied heavily on candlelight in order to illuminate its lavish interior furnishings.

About the same time as the founding of St. Oswald's the manor house was being developed close to the original place chosen by the Romans at Kingsholm. This manor house was known as a palace by the time of Edward the Confessor and it was a place where important councils were held. A hoard of coins found locally was so large that it was deduced that they represented the taxes collected from the inhabitants of a very wide surrounding area.

During the 11th century Gloucester's fortunes improved tremendously. Evidence

*The Norman lead font in Lady Chapel, Gloucester Cathedral*

*The sad remains of St Oswald's Priory*

suggests that silversmiths, potters, glass craftsmen and iron workers were developing their trades in addition to the regular productivity of cobblers and weavers. By 1086 there was a market and a Mint and a system of freehold property which of course encouraged an active market in property. After the arrival of the Normans the Saxon nobles were dispossessed and the new master was the Earl of Hereford, William Fitz-Osbern, who ruled over much of western England. The Sheriff of the County of Gloucester was Roger de Pitres who headed the family destined to dominate Gloucester for many years. A building programme was started including the construction of a castle with which the town could be controlled and the local countryside subdued. It was a "motte and bailey" affair which was more or less a standard design of the period, a mound of earth with a wooden tower on top, all defended by stout timber fencing. Roger, in addition to being County Sheriff, became Constable of the castle and naturally the military backing he had achieved made the collection of revenues by his forces a quite straightforward procedure.

The older Roman gateways to the town were rebuilt and after the appointment of Serlo as Abbot of Gloucester in 1072 work began some 17 years later on a major undertaking for which the Normans were famous, the building of a new Abbey church. Earlier there had been a Saxon church which had been damaged during the Norman invasion but the Normans as always thought big when thinking of Abbeys and this, the Cathedral of Gloucester, was big!

Walter was the son of Roger de Pitres and Miles was his grandson so it was decided that Walter and Miles would jointly rebuild the castle. The earlier construction of earth and timber was levelled and during the early 1100s, on a site just to the west, a stone replacement was built. At about the same time as the castle was built the old Roman quayside, which had become useless due to the movement to the west of the river, was demolished and no doubt much of the material was incorporated into the new building. The County Prison today stands on the site of the castle.

The trouble and strife caused to England by the accession of Stephen to the throne is mentioned later in this book at Woodstock but Gloucester with its castle became involved in this controversy. Miles, grandson of Roger de Pitres, who was by now Constable of the castle and County Sheriff, had in 1138 in Gloucester received Stephen as King. A year later, however, Matilda, the daughter of Henry I, landed in England and Miles was one of those who chose allegiance to her. By 1141 he was fighting on her behalf when Stephen was captured and since she was at Gloucester the prisoner was at first brought to Gloucester castle, later being transferred to Bristol. Matilda sped off to London, possibly to claim the throne, but she was defeated and at Oxford (hence the connection with Woodstock) she endowed Miles with the Earldom of Hereford. After losing a further battle she hastened back again to the security of Gloucester while Miles tried to secure for her, adequate financial support. Following his death in a hunting accident in 1143 disagreements surfaced as to the suitability of the burial place for such an important man. Finally he was buried at a monastery of his founding, namely Llanthory-by-Gloucester.

During the wars with the Welsh in the early 12th century this monastery, set admit the Black Mountains, was hard pressed and depended heavily on the Bishop of Hereford for support. Miles gave them land close to Gloucester, the monks were transferred and built an abbey church in 1137. Following his initial gift of land he bequeathed on the abbey further churches within the town, the castle chapel and the Quedgeley fishery. After this the Bishop of Hereford had little success in persuading the monks to return to the Black Mountains of Wales and consequently Llanthory-by-Gloucester developed and prospered and at its peak it was without doubt one of the richest of medieval England's monasteries. Today little remains of this once splendid and influential building except for the 15th century tithe barn which is the earliest known medieval brick construction in Gloucester.

Roger, the son of Miles, lost the Earldom

*The Old West Gate beyond the Hooper Monument*

inherited from his father in 1155, with the result that the great castle and all that it had stood for passed at last into the hands of the King, Henry II.

By now the town had spread outside the town walls and eventually outer gates were built. The church of St. Owen was founded in 1087 in a former suburb. In the west a new bridge, the Foreign Bridge, crossed the Severn in the 1100s and a little later Nicholas Walred, a priest, built the Westgate Bridge. While this was under construction a freeholder of the town loaned a nearby house to accommodate the workmen; this later became a travellers'

*Of the few remaining timber framed buildings in Gloucester, this one in Hare Lane is a fine example*

hospital and is said to be the forerunner of St. Bartholomew's. A new bridge was built on this site in 1972 and during the excavations a number of the original bridge spans came to light.

By the early 1400s Gloucester had developed quite considerably. The Abbey had many pilgrims to marvel at its architecture and to pay homage to the martyrdom at Berkeley castle in 1327 of Edward II. At the time of the King's 'disappearance' the government had made no admission that a murder had been committed, let alone by who. Instead it had put about rumours that the King had passed away due to natural causes. Thus a feeling of suspicion developed among the people of medieval England and the country as a whole grew impatient that no proper explanation regarding his death was forthcoming. Some could not believe that the King was dead and preferred to believe that he had been whisked away at the dead of night, perhaps to Corfe Castle in Dorset or even abroad. One story tells of his escape to Italy where a refuge was provided by the Pope at the Castello di Melazzo in northern Italy.

Unpopular during his lifetime he was regarded by many after his murder as a saint and his body, buried at Gloucester Abbey, soon became a steady means of income generation. Soon the Abbey constructed local accommodation for its guests in the form of inns and hostelries. The New Inn, for instance, is still in existence and is said to be the best example of a galleried inn in the country. In its heyday it accommodated a couple of hundred guests within its dormitories.

Other old inns and coaching houses abound in Gloucester, amongst them The Fleece Hotel, in Westgate Street, which dates from around 1500. It was originally built by the Abbey and following the Dissolution it became the property of the

Cathedral. At the peak of the Cotswold wool trade it was known as The Golden Fleece but by the late 1700s it fell into disrepair and remained vacant for a number of years. Around 1800 the church sold it off since which time it has been privately owned. Below the Fleece is an old storage area with a tunnel vaulted roof held aloft by stout circular pillars; today it is a unique bar area in this historic building.

By the mid 1300s the trades and industries of the town were flourishing and trade associations and guilds abounded. One of the strongest was the tanners guild whose members functioned in Tanner's Lane, later known as Hare Lane, and the most important was the guild of the wool trades. Gloucester was also becoming recognised at this time for its iron trades, Broadsmith and Longsmith streets both being names of former iron working areas of the city. In and around Northgate Street weavers and glove makers pursued their crafts, while mercers and butchers abounded in Westgate Street. Cloth and corn were important exports carried in small vessels to be offloaded for Ireland and continental Europe at Bristol where they were reloaded onto larger sea going vessels. Meanwhile the numerous churches, monasteries and most of all the Abbey had become incredibly rich and powerful, as indeed had many of the churches throughout the land. However, within a four year period from 1536 the situation was drastically changed and the Dissolution was in progress, by order of Henry VIII. As a result a new diocese was created with the Abbey of St. Peter's church as the Cathedral served by a college of secular canons. This resulted in the nearby names of College Court and College Street.

The Abbey's property was largely inherited by the new Cathedral but much of the Abbey's other properties went to those rich enough to be able to bid for it. While some owners disregarded any charitable obligations inherent in the ownership of their new properties, others such as Thomas Bell, whilst providing himself with a further means of income, did in fact share some of the benefits with other less fortunate than himself. He had purchased Blackfriars church complete with all its properties in addition to much monastic property in Gloucester. He had the ends of the church knocked out and an upper floor installed and by adding new windows he created a very sizable and handsome house for himself. The former dining hall and its ancillary buildings were converted into a cloth factory providing work for a few hundred people. Near the south gate and close to the site of the former Saxon chapel of St. Kyneburgh he built an almshouse for six persons. On his death in 1566 he left money for the city's poor and those inmates of Gloucester prisons. In his lifetime he had been Mayor three times and was knighted twenty years before his death.

The schools of Gloucester in those days were provided for by other benefactors, one of which was Richard Pate who had, on behalf of Henry VIII, surveyed much of the properties before the Dissolution. With this prior knowledge he was of course better equipped to bid for the choicest pieces, which he did, but he also endowed the grammar school. Similarly when John Cook departed this life in 1528, his wife became a wealthy woman and was able, at the Dissolution, to buy up much of the estate of the Llanthony Priory. This she used to endow the school of St. Mary de Crypt in Southgate Street.

Following the Dissolution the town was deeply divided as regards its religious beliefs. These differences became highlighted in 1550 with the appointment of Bishop Hooper to the town. He had spent some of his earlier years in Switzerland where he became influenced by the Lutheran doctrine; he also had a wife who was a Protestant. In 1553 Queen Mary of Scots ascended the throne and as a Catholic one of her first tasks was to attempt to crush the Protestant movement by force. Hooper, as an eminent figure in a position of power, was tried for treason and sentenced to death. He was returned to Gloucester in 1555 and is said to have stayed in Lower Westgate Street, in the building which is now home to the Folk Museum, before being burnt at the stake in St. Mary's Square, where there is now a Monument to him.

By the early 1600s Puritanism was growing steadily in Gloucester for it was a town struggling with rising poverty and the appeal of godly discipline and public control looked very attractive to those who had next to nothing. The Archbishop of Canterbury was naturally quite opposed to this attitude which was gathering momentum well in advance of the disputes between King and Parliament; Gloucester was becoming strongly Parliamentarian.

By 1643 Cirencester had fallen to Prince Rupert but at Gloucester, although not ready for an onslaught, Lt. Colonel Massey who was in command, had refused the demands to surrender the city to the King. With the fall of Bristol to the King's troops in July of the same year Gloucester stood alone as the only Parliamentarian city of any significance in the west of England. By 10th August and with 30,000 of his troops surrounding the city Charles I offered to pardon all inhabitants if they surrendered there and then. They refused and so began the famous siege of Gloucester. The Royalists rightly felt that since they now held Bristol, to take Gloucester as well would reduce the need to hold forces in Wales and it would give them control of the River Severn. Further, the iron foundries situated in the Forest of Dean would be a most welcome addition to the King's arsenal.

The Royalists attacked with artillery and siege engines from the south and east, while the defending garrison adapted a scorched earth policy and burnt down the suburbs outside the old walls thereby giving the enemy as little cover as possible. By 7th September the Earl of Essex leading his columns of relief forces made his triumphal entry into Gloucester. The defenders having lost about 35 dead had but a few barrels of gunpowder left and the siege was lifted. The south gate to the city had been so badly damaged that it required rebuilding and over its gate an inscription was raised, 'A city assaulted by man but saved by God.'

By 1660 Charles II was on the throne and with due regard to the city's sympathies of

*A stunning piece of timber frame architecture, Hooper's House*

a few years earlier he did his best to ensure that the Royalist course would not be opposed again. Local commissioners appointed on behalf of the King were required amongst other things to see to it that the city walls were well breached and the gates taken down. During the same year, however, the Market House in Southgate Street was rebuilt and five years later the old church of St. Oswald's was demolished and the stone used to build a barley market in Eastgate Street. Curiously a statue of Charles II was erected about this time but during the mid 1700s it disappeared, only to reappear about 200 years later at Westbury-on-Severn. It now stands in a garden near Three Locks Lane.

It was during the later half of the 17th century that Gloucester developed two quite specialist and different industries: one was the manufacture of metal pins which were sold all over England and the other was foundry working, especially bell casting. The Rudhall family became well known throughout the land for their church bells, having satisfied customers in well over 100 parishes before 1740.

While mentioning church bells one might think of church, then Sunday Schools. One of the founding fathers of the Sunday School movement in England is generally accepted as being Robert Raikes, who rightly felt that these schools must, in addition to religious education, give basic instruction in reading and writing. This of course was all that the children of the poor could hope for as most worked long hours as cheap labour. Raikes was born at Lady Bellgate House which was one of those fine homes built for the wealthy around 1700 in the centre of Gloucester. During recent years it was restored by the Gloucester Civic Trust after narrowly missing demolition. Similarly restored is the nearby Bearland House in Longsmith Street.

In the 1700s brick became very fashionable throughout the country as a new building material and was frequently being used to reface the front elevations of older properties. Older timber framed houses such as Winfields and St. Nicholas' House in Westgate Street are good examples of this "false fronting".

Gloucester is remarkably well endowed with parish churches, all of which are of interest to the visitor having an interest in history and the time to explore. In Northgate Street is the church of St. John the Baptist, the nave of which dates from the 18th century whilst the tower and spire are four centuries older. Both John Wesley and George Whitfield who was born in the city in 1714 preached here. There are three churches of St. Mary, one of which is St. Mary de Crypt in Southgate Street where Norman stonework is to be seen in the crypt. In the main this church with its central tower was rebuilt during the 15th century; this work is usually attributed to Henry Dere, the prior of Llanthory. The previously mentioned Sunday School founder Robert Raikes is remembered here with a monument. The founders of the Crypt Grammar School, John and Joan Coake, have memorial brasses dating from 1544.

*Victoria Basin, Gloucester Docks*

A Norman south doorway is to be seen at St. Nicholas's in Westgate Street together with transitional arches from the same period. The Perpendicular tower has side aisles extended from each side of it. A coronet and pinnacles replaced the spire during the late 18th century.

St. Margaret's Chapel in London Road was originally used as a leper hospital and dates from the 13th century. A second leper hospital once stood in the same road but the 12th century St. Mary Magdalene, which was once the hospital's chapel, is all that is left today.

In Southgate Street, just above the Edwardian shop front of No. 5, is a most interesting mechanical clock with five figures which represent Old Father Time amidst England, Scotland, Wales and Ireland.

At the corner of Eastgate Street and Southgate Street stands St. Michael's Tower. It dates from the 15th century and from the time of its completion until the outbreak of hostilities in 1939, apart from a break during the 19th century, the curfew bell tolled from it. From the mid 1700s trading times of the markets were rung out from the tower and since the mid 1980s the Tourist Information Office has been based in the tower.

A visit to Gloucester is not complete without some time spent at the Docks. A few of the wharfs are still in commercial use by coasters and pleasure craft but the hustle and bustle of years gone by is no longer present. Today the old warehouses and basins are, in the main, museum pieces preserved for the benefit of the visitor and developed as apartments and the like. Since the earliest times the River Severn was important to the growth of trade between Bristol and the manufacturing towns of the Midlands but it was Elizabeth I who in 1580 granted Gloucester the formal status of a port. For generations sailing vessels known as trows and having a shallow draught

*The Cathedral watches over Gloucester Docks*

conveyed cargoes along the river. Many of these vessels were only able to pass the narrow winding stretch close to Gloucester on certain high tides, so difficult was the river to navigate. In order to overcome this problem work on the Gloucester and Berkeley Canal was commenced by Robert Mylne in 1793 during the heady days of England's "Canal Mania". Canals were being constructed at that time all over the country. Many proved to be successful but others, for a variety of reasons, were not. The Gloucester and Berkeley Canal turned out to be something of a compromise, its final length and route being a much modified conclusion of the earlier project and it was eventually completed under the supervision of Thomas Fletcher in 1827. During this rather drawn out business a horse drawn railway, similar to that operating from Moreton-in-Marsh, was installed to connect Cheltenham with Gloucester's main dock basin and by 1812 the lock was operational. Roadstone and timber at that time were two of the main cargoes carried from further down the estuary but perhaps the most valuable cargo was coal from the Forest of Dean. Soon an extra barge arm was dug out which enabled the sea going vessels to gain exclusive use of the main basin with its warehousing facilities.

With the opening of the canal local merchants were importing via their new local waterway system, thus the older system, using trans-shipment at Bristol with its high port charges, was bypassed. Most cargo was being off loaded directly onto the smaller narrow boats which carried the cargoes up the river and via the maze of inland waterways and locks, right into the industrial heartland of England. As business boomed new warehouses sprang up and an engine house to power the pumping system from the River Severn was built while large timber quays with adjacent

storage yards were developed along the canal. By 1849 the Victoria Dock was opened to the east of the Main Basin and a canal-like cut linked them together.

About this time it was decided that the horse drawn narrow gauge railway system was out of date and the Midland Railway duly extended a standard gauge branch line to the south end of Bakers Quay with an additional branch to the east of the main docking complex. Within a year or two a branch from South Wales linked with a further new quay to the canal's west side and it was these lines that presented the greatest competition to the canal and river routes to the Midlands.

As technology advanced and with the ever increasing size of merchant shipping it was apparent by the second half of the 19th century that Gloucester was experiencing difficulties in accommodating the latest, most economical vessels. At Sharpness therefore in 1874 a new entrance and dock was opened, the cargoes of large vessels being transferred to barges and conveyed up the canal.

King Edward's Gate in College Street was once part of the western tower of the Abbey's lynch gate and was built by Edward I. In 1327 King Edward II's body was received here by the Abbot prior to its internment in the Abbey. The gateway was much modified during the early 19th century and obviously during more recent times a rather grand gateway has been added.

During the 13th century the Cathedral Close was enclosed by stout stone walls, part of which acted as the city's defensive walls. A number of fine buildings were erected in the Close following the Abbey's dissolution and the area as a whole has been little altered during the last two centuries.

The Church House dates from the 13th century and it is where important visitors to the abbey were entertained, Henry VIII and Anne Boleyn being amongst them. Dating from the same period is the lovely old gateway of St. Mary's. The timber framed structure is 16th century and is built on top of the undercroft of 13th century walls. Similarly constructed, but about a century older, is the Parliament Room where, in 1378, Richard II held parliament.

Whilst it is by no means the largest of England's cathedrals, Gloucester Cathedral is considered to be one of the country's most beautiful examples of ecclesiastical architecture. The eastern arm of the Abbey Church, as it was then, was dedicated on 15th July 1100. Completed almost entirely in pale cream Cotswold stone from Painswick and Minchinhampton, the first impression of Gloucester Cathedral is one of Perpendicular architecture. This is due to its almost overpowering 225ft high tower which is covered with louvred openings and blank arcading set in tiers. Topped with pinnacles linked with open parapets, from a distance it has a certain delicate appearance of filigree. The main entrance is by way of the south porch where the tower's pinnacles and parapets are repeated on a smaller scale, the niches having 19th century figures by Redfern. Inside are fine stone panels and inner doors with Norman hinges. Inside the nave the arcades are supported by huge circular Norman columns with slim, round capitals. Here are an abundance of notable features. The celestery windows and those in the north aisle contain some medieval glass; the glass in the main, however, is Victorian. Of a host of memorials perhaps one which is outstanding is the free-standing figure at the rear of the nave of Dr. Edward Jenner, the Gloucestershire inventor of the smallpox vaccine, and by the same sculptor, R.W. Sievier, is the bust of the prison reformer Sir George Onesiphorus Paul, which is in the south aisle.

The Choir was reconstructed, after the burial of Edward II, with tall celestory windows together with the addition of the east window. In the south ambulatory of the Choir and just opposite to the 15th century cope chest is a wooden effigy of the eldest son of William the Conqueror, Robert, Duke of Normandy. When his father died in 1087 he was granted the Dukedom of Normandy but convinced that the throne of England should be his he fought his two brothers William Rufus and Henry. Unfortunately he lost the fight and was captured in 1106, spending the remaining 28 years of his life as a prisoner in Cardiff Castle. He was buried in the Chapter House of the Cathedral but not before the high altar, as he had requested. The effigy was damaged by Cromwellians during the Civil War but later repaired and replaced in the Cathedral. As a complete contrast, and for me far more touching, is the very small and simple stone cross close to the war memorial chapel. As a 15 year old I well remember reading of the Glorious Gloucesters, as they became known, at the Battle of the Imjin River in Korea during April 1951. The cross was carved by Lt. Colonel J.P. Carne, V.C., D.S.O., whilst held captive in North Korea, and on completion it was used at services held at the prison camp.

Go from the ambulatory and into the Lady Chapel via the vestibule, at the centre of which is a font made of lead. It was presented to the Cathedral over 50 years ago but originally dates from 1140 and came from a ruined church in the Wye Valley. The Lady Chapel is the most recent part of the whole building. Modern by comparison with the remainder, it was nevertheless completed before 1500 and is unique in having small transcepts formed on each side by the singing galleries above the chantry chapels.

The cloisters of Gloucester Cathedral are amongst the finest in Europe and famed for their fan vaulting. If you stand at one end and gaze down the length of just one side it will be obvious why this is so, for the effect is almost as if viewing an avenue of trees with branches reaching out and meeting overhead, and all of this was completed before 1412

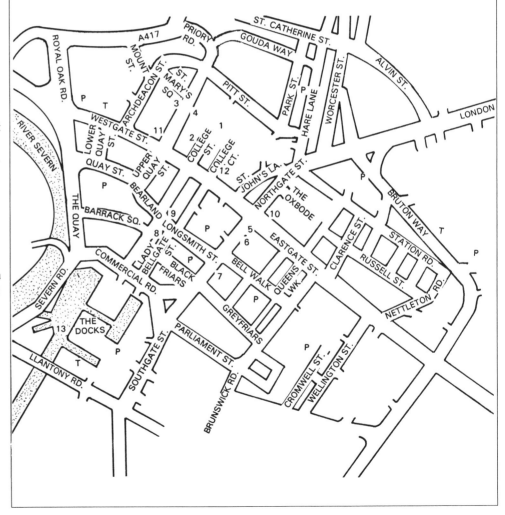

**GLOUCESTER**

P  Parking
T  Toilets
1  Cathedral
2  King Edward's Gate
3  Bishop Hooper's Monument
4  St. Mary's Gateway
5  St. Michael's Tower
6  The Mechanical Clock
7  St. Mary de Crypt
8  Bearland House
9  Lady Bellgate House
10  The New Inn
11  St. Nicholas' House
12  The Beatrix Potter Shop
13  The Docks

# 11: Malmesbury

*Malmesbury Abbey*

To the north are the high pasture lands filled with grazing sheep for which the Cotswolds is renowned, while to the south across the flat lands of the Avon valley with its fields of dairy cattle are the Wiltshire Downs, and at the confluence of two small streams is Malmesbury. The streams, both Avons, have flowed from different directions, one from Sherston and the other from Tetbury. Here they surround this huge piece of rocky outcrop with its level top, above which the town skyline is overlooked by the Abbey. Throughout history this high vantage point must have proved to be a natural fortress with its commanding views across the surrounding countryside and its natural moat. The two Avons nearly meet to the west of the town, then separate to flow round it on the northern and southern edges to meet completely on the southeastern side.

Unlike so many of the Cotswold towns, Malmesbury has no connection with the Romans for no Roman-British remains have been found hereabouts. With the old Roman road, the Fosse Way, passing only a mile or two to the north of the town, this is surprising. One theory is that this high position was inhabited long before the Romans arrived in England and it may have

*The south porch, Malmesbury Abbey*

been that the Romans, with their own high standard of civilisation, found the natives of this area too primitive to warrant their interest. A connection with and a description of such a rough and unsophisticated population could possibly be found in the description 'wild' - it could be that this was described as 'Wylt', thus in later years the county name of Wyltshire evolved.

With the arrival of the Saxons shortly after AD570 today's counties of Somerset, Wiltshire and Hampshire became Wessex and about 30 years later Maildulph, a Celtic monk, set up a tiny monastery where he educated the sons of the upper classes. Aldhelm, a senior student, succeeded Maildulph to become the first Abbot of the newly formed Abbey during the AD670's. He was a relation of Ina, King of Wessex, the connection with whom naturally added to his prestige and influence as a scholar who had studied at Canterbury and visited Pope Sergius I. The Pope in turn and as a tremendous honour placed the Abbey under papal jurisdiction thereby relinquishing any right of control locally. Aldhelm built a number of churches in the vicinity, the most famous of those still standing being the lovely Saxon church at Bradford-on-Avon. It seems that he was not just a wise churchman and talented architect but also something of an extrovert. One who, we are led to believe, was not above speaking to the ordinary people in the street, and when he attracted a reasonable crowd he would usher them into church for divine service. He became the Bishop of Sherbourne in AD705 but died four years later. Thus the foundations of the great abbey and consequently the town of Malmesbury were laid.

It is said that the town took its name from a combination of these two early churchmen, Maildulph and Aldhelm. Initially in AD683 the name was 'Maeldubesberg' and was later modified to 'Maldemesburuh' from where the transition to its present one is a simple step.

King Alfred the Great had strong connections with the town, becoming the town patron and granting the town its first charter, it is claimed, in AD880. The more readily accepted date however was in AD924 during the reign of his son Edward the Elder. After many years of skirmishing and sackings Edward was joined by his sister who was known as the 'Lady of the Mercians' and together their combined armies proved to be a formidable fighting force against the Danes. It is generally accepted that it was in recognition of the fighting spirit displayed in the endless campaigns that Edward reaffirmed the wishes of his father that Malmesbury's charter should be granted. But it was Athelston, grandson of Alfred, who was chosen by election to be the first Saxon King of England and the Patron King of Malmesbury. He became a renowned warrior, churchman and governor and was acknowledged throughout the Kingdom and beyond for his library and works of art. He gave the land known as Kings Heath or Malmesbury Common to the people of the town and additional land to the Abbey. He also donated land for the building of St.

Paul's Cathedral and was involved with the construction of the Minsters of Beverley and York.

During the time of Edward the Confessor a great fire swept through Malmesbury and much of the town, being of timber construction, like the Abbey, was destroyed. At the time the King and the Bishop of Sherbourne agreed that the new stone building under construction should be combined with the Bishopric. The monks unfortunately disagreed with this proposal, which would have provided the opportunity for Malmesbury and not Salisbury to develop as the county's Cathedral city.

One of the more light hearted tales associated with the town dates from about AD1000 when a monk by the name of Elmer became the earliest recorded human to fly. He was something of an astronomer and a dabbler in geometry who is reputed to have built some kind of winged contraption which would enable him to fly like the birds. It is said that with the aid of his flying apparatus he leapt from an Abbey tower and glided down to earth; unfortunately due to cross winds he crash landed. This resulted in him being lame for the rest of his days but no doubt pleased to have lived to tell the tale.

When the conquering Normans marched across the land William I reaffirmed the earlier charter and his wife extended the fair which had always been held in respect of the Abbey's founder, Aldhelm, from five to eight days' duration. She was, it seems, a perfect lady and the historian of the period, William of Malmesbury, who was the Abbey's librarian, undoubtedly held her in great esteem. Unbeknown to him, however, she was enjoying an affair with one of the King's nobles. When her husband heard of the affair he saw to it that the Queen's lover had an 'accident' and later, following

*The Market Cross*

*Above: The Old Goose Bridge at Malmesbury*          *Below: St John's Hospital*

the death of the King, she duly had the church at Avering, near Tetbury, constructed as a memorial to her former lover's memory. A romance perhaps not dissimilar to that of fair Rosamund and the King many years later which took place at Woodstock.

By 1100 the Bishop of Salisbury seems to have been continually aggressive toward his brothers at Malmesbury Abbey so as part of the town's walled defence system he decided to build a castle close against the west end of the Abbey. This he did in order to threaten and annoy them but during the reign of King John it was pulled down. The garrison had, amongst other things, taken to interfering with the supply of water to the Abbey and as a result Pope Alexander agreed to the Abbot excommunicating those concerned. The fine old Bell Hotel, which stands close by, still contains a few of the former castle remains in the form of extremely thick walls and a Norman arch. The land beneath is said to be riddled with passages while under the kitchen a vaulted chamber was said to contain eight coffins of stone.

Malmesbury reached a peak of prosperity during the 1400s and right into the following century. The woollen trade had developed throughout earlier generations and at this time it progressed from strength to strength. The close proximity to a ready supply of running water was the key to milling and it is said that at one time there were eight mills along the rivers close to the town. Of course while the town prospered and grew so did the Abbey and vast areas of land and to a great extent the lives of those who lived upon them were controlled by the Abbey of Malmesbury. Toward the end of the 15th century the Abbey was beginning to weaken both in the discipline and dedication of the monks and consequently through neglect the structure itself. As if to

herald the decline that was imminently approaching, the great spire, which was higher than that at Salisbury, collapsed. The last Abbot, John Selwyn, carried on with a handful of monks until in 1539 the end came as part of Henry VIII's Dissolution of the Monasteries. For almost eight and a half centuries the Benedictines had held sway at Malmesbury and with their demise came grave unemployment for the people of Malmesbury.

To their rescue, but particularly to line his own pockets, came William Stumpe, a rich clothier who owned the original Wynyards Mill and paid £1,500 to Henry VIII's steward for the Abbey's outbuildings and its surrounding lands. He was something of an entrepreneur who saw an opportunity to use cheap labour. He turned the nave of the Abbey into a factory, filling it with looms, and proceeded to churn out a high quality cloth which became well known throughout Europe. He grew very rich very quickly and his son married the daughter of Henry VIII's steward. Stumpe became a Protestant and represented Malmesbury in Parliament and when trade was declining in 1541 he returned the abbey to the town as the Parish church.

During the turbulent days of the English Civil War the position of Malmesbury on the main highway between the southwest and Oxford made it strategically important. In spite of Charles I regranting the town's charter in acknowledgement of its achievements in weaving, in the main the townsfolk decided to side with Cromwell. The town was captured by the King's forces early in 1643. At this time some of the old town walls were still intact and had not entirely been destroyed during earlier centuries, thus the town, with water on three sides, was readily defendable. Barely a month later Sir William Waller and the Parliamentarians arrived and were held off by the defenders' musket men for a time but inevitably the town fell to the attackers. By April Prince Rupert attacked and found it to be defended by only 120 troops so it became a Royalist town for a short period, then when the garrison was ordered to Reading the town was occupied by the Cromwellians. Prince Rupert and the Royalists duly returned to take Malmesbury en route to Bristol but when the King arrived the Mayor and residents were so sick of their town being a pawn that they understandably gave him the cold shoulder. A year of occupation by the Royalists followed but during the early summer of 1644 Colonel Massey had been ordered to

*The Old Tolsey Gate*

re-take Malmesbury for the Parliamentarians. Massey requested that the King's men surrender. They refused, there followed Malmesbury's final battle of the war and it once again returned to the Parliamentarian side.

Visitors from the 'New World' are always interested to find connections with whichever part of the 'Old World' their forefathers had emigrated from. Here at Malmesbury there are two very famous connections, one being with William Penn, the founder of Pennsylvania, and the other with Abraham Lincoln whose mother came from Malmesbury. A few miles from the town is the village of Minty and it was from here that the Penn family originated, their residence being known as the Mansells.

Architecturally, one of the finest houses in Malmesbury is the Abbey House which was, until recent years, the home of an Anglican order of nuns. The house dates from the 16th century and was originally built by William Stumpe in the place formerly occupied by the house of the Abbot. It stands on a Norman base and part of the garden is where the High Altar, Cloisters and Lady Chapel of the Abbey stood before the Dissolution.

The visitor may be intrigued by the tall square tower which sprouts from one of the cottages in Haynes Lane and is best viewed from Oxford Street. This is the Tower House and was part of the town walls and defence system mentioned earlier. It is said that at one time Henry VIII was entertained here; no doubt the buildings beneath and surrounding it were very different then.

In days gone by the Lords of the Manor kept doves and pigeons in a dove cote or pigeon cote, the derivation of which was 'Culver House'. This building, three storeys high with fine mullioned windows, on the right near the bottom of Black Hill, was the dwelling place of the servants of the old

Manor House. At the bottom of Black Hill the steps lead down to the old Goose Bridge beyond which is Wynyards Mill just past a row of terraced houses, once the homes and workplaces of the town's basket makers.

At the junction of Lower High Street and St. John's Street stands what remains of the old Priory of St. John of Jerusalem and across St. John's Bridge are the old Silk Mills. They have during their long lifetime been used as corn, wool and silk mills.

The streets of Malmesbury all have a certain charm for the visitor but without doubt the centre of attraction for most people is the Abbey. As already mentioned it was used as a huge factory by William Stumpe following the Dissolution. After he had finished with it he restored it to the standard we see today and the nave, where his main production area was, has little changed for 600 years. Typical of the Romanesque period of Norman architecture, huge circular pillars support arches which are slightly pointed. Above the arches small round columns support four small arches of the triforium while round arches with chevron mouldings are above. Certain modifications were made during the 14th century; in the north aisle these included the addition of a large window above the cloister roof. On the south side the 'watching loft' is a rather harsh looking cabin which protrudes into the upper section of the nave. It is thought that this may have been a kind of sentry look-out position from where watch could be kept on all those viewing the Abbey's treasures and visiting the shrine of Aldhelm. The Victorians restored much of the stone vaulting of the roof, guilding a number of bosses. A king, queen, knight, lady and court jester are represented here.

When the Abbey's spire collapsed about AD1500, the arch above the chancel screen of stone was filled in, thus providing a new east wall. The coat of arms of Henry VII

along with other decorations of the period are still visible on the cornice. The choir stalls and pulpit are much more recent, dating from 1928.

In the north aisle is the medieval table top tomb of the Saxon King Athelstan and on the other side of the screen are memorials to the family of William Stumpe. At the eastern end of the south aisle is the chapel of St. Aldhelm where he is represented by a small statue in wood. Outside the chapel is the parish chest of 1638.

Unusually the Abbey has two fonts: the one in the south aisle is 15th century and came from St. Mary's at Westport, the other font in the nave's west end is 17th century. The William Scott Luce memorial window is the work of Burne-Jones and William Morris whose associations with Chipping Campden and Broadway are mentioned under those towns.

The great arches which supported the lantern tower and the spire before AD1500 can still be seen behind the south transept outside the abbey, but the porch is perhaps the most interesting part of the abbey. The beautiful carved Norman arches of the doorway depict some of the Bible stories, the Creation, Old Testament and the life of Christ. On the inside of the porch the carvings of the Apostles are considered to be amongst the finest in the land. Above all this Norman splendour is a room known as the Parvise where gunpowder was stored during Malmesbury's turbulent days in the Civil War. At one time it became, like other such rooms, the local school but nowadays it houses the Abbey's treasures of manuscripts, books and prints.

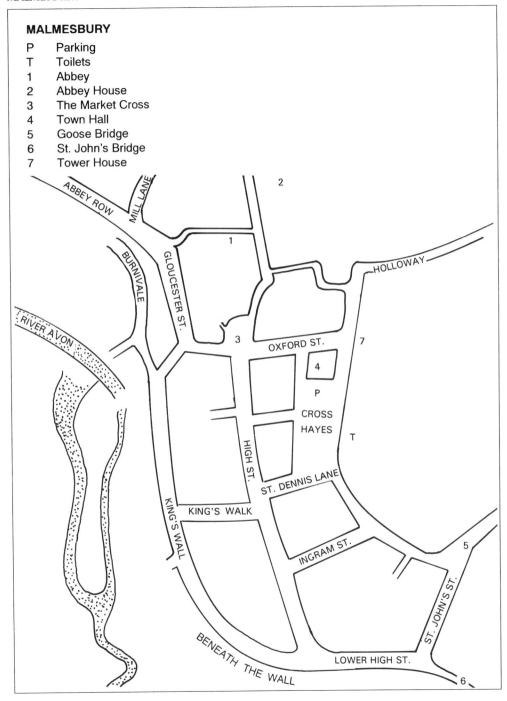

**MALMESBURY**

P   Parking
T   Toilets
1   Abbey
2   Abbey House
3   The Market Cross
4   Town Hall
5   Goose Bridge
6   St. John's Bridge
7   Tower House

# 12: Minchinhampton

*Minchinhampton seen from Butt Street*

The Church of the Holy Trinity at Minchinhampton, with its central tower beneath a truncated spire, looks down across the Market Square to the High Street as it slopes away westward. It is not the most stunning of Cotswold churches, nor is it one of the oldest, but it has a number of interesting features and gives the impression of being well cared for. It was restored and updated in 1842 and until that time there stood four Norman arches on the north side of the nave with a number of small blocked up windows from the same period. Sadly the 'restorers' decided to demolish them together with other parts of the building which dated from the 14th and 16th centuries. Today's nave and chancel therefore are barely 150 years old while the handsome tower and transepts are 14th century.

The Nave is high and lofty with a very attractively decorated ceiling which was completed in 1962. The memorials, which are pre 1842, are mainly to the former Lords of the Manor and builders of Gatcombe Park, namely the Sheppard's. Perhaps the most unusual memorial is on the east wall. Jeremiah Buck was a mercer in Minchinhampton and a Parliamentarian who, it seemed, made a habit of attacking men of the cloth. In 1643 he was reported to have attacked the Rector of Minchinhampton and his daughter who intercepted the violence. Later Mr. Buck married into one of the local families of aristocrats, his dubious past conveniently forgotten as his new father-in-law entertained Charles I and his entourage during the King's siege of Gloucester.

The south transept which dates from the early 1300s measures 40ft long x 60ft wide x 40ft high and is a most interesting piece of architecture. Its high pitched roof appears to have little support except for a series of stone ribs but outside are a number of buttresses which take most of the weight. This part of the original church must have been very attractive during the 14th century as the floors would have been covered with tiles similar to the sample displayed on the west wall and whole interior coloured with the traces one can decipher on the archway which leads into the south transept. The Victorians, with all their good intentions, have much to answer for.

The church's rather unusual spire with its coronet of pinnacles dates from 1563 when the top half of the original spire was removed to save it from collapse.

Over the years the town itself developed near the crossing place of old roadways.

Tetbury Street runs east and West End goes in the opposite direction of the crossing with Well Hill (which leads down to the town's old water source) and the bottom of the High Street. At the top of the High Street the road opens out to form the Market Square where in 1698 the handsome Market House was constructed as were the cottages which adjoin the churchyard and face the war memorial. Naturally the most substantial of the town's architecture is situated in the High Street where some of the buildings were formerly coaching inns.

At the top of the High Street on the west side the Crown Inn has nine bays of sash windows and dates from the 18th century, while lower down Arden House and Cottage combined have a 16th century front. On the corner of Tetbury Street is the former White Hart Inn, now a large gabled building dating from the 17th century with 18th century modifications. More recently it has been sub-divided and is now used as two different business premises. An unusual piece of architecture is on the south side of Tetbury Street where the visitor will find that parts of what appears to be a stone fireplace have been used as decoration for the exterior of the building dated 1682. Possibly the fireplace was too cumbersome to install inside. The house is certainly a most distinctive building and is unique in its appearance. If the visitor cares to stroll along West End, near the junction with Dr. Brown's Road will be seen the long terrace of houses built in 1833 by David Ricardo. Park Terrace is a series of sturdy stone houses comprising a ground and upper floor, each house having a dormer in the attic.

Until the early 1700s Minchinhampton, like the not too distant towns of Fairford, Tetbury and Cirencester, was still an important wool producing town but as the business declined in the south and developed in the north of England other places in Gloucestershire developed new industries as a means of income. Minchinhampton at this time seems to have pursued no other main avenue of income and so became bypassed and continued to exist as a rural town of lesser importance. In the main the "wool" families of Minchinhampton had not the vast riches of some of those in other Cotswold towns and consequently they lacked the necessary wealth to become owners of large estates when the wool trade declined.

The other local industry was quarrying which was carried out both on and around

*The church of Holy Trinity*

*At the top of the High Street*

the Common. The Great Oolite or upper stratum was used as the building stone and the finer grained Inferior Oolite or lower stratum was better suited to interior use. Today the many scars left by this quarrying can readily be seen on the Common, while just to the south at Balls Green is where much of the stone was quarried to provide material from which the Houses of Parliament were built. To the north the Burleigh quarry was owned by Gloucester Cathedral and it was from this source that the stone required for this magnificent building was supplied.

The vast Commons of Minchinhampton are today the property of the National Trust and cover an area in excess of 600 acres. Rodborough Common which borders the Minchinhampton land is also a large grazing area. Unlike other areas of Cotswold common land these never were enclosed, thus we still see cattle and horses grazing close to the town. The only deterrent to the animals on the main roads which cross the Commons and on the driveways of houses close to this grazing land are cattle grids. There are no hedges or fences. Hundreds of years ago there was a great deal of woodland around Minchinhampton and in 1086 the Domesday records showed an area of 2 x $^1/_2$ league of timberlands and eight mills at Minchinhampton.

Locally the best known part of the Commons is at the junction of six roads where the sign reads, "Tom Long's Post". Some say that it was usual to bury those who had committed suicide at such a point, but others say that this is where convicted highwaymen were hung. Tom Long is said to have been a highwayman who was hung here but there are people who dispute this. Possibly he was a local weaver who, for unknown reasons, committed suicide. Over the years strange images have been seen at different places on the Common and as recently as 1977 two men were said to have witnessed a ghostly coach crossing the Rodborough Common by way of the old coach route which linked Gloucester to London.

Many of the scars and undulations which are visible all over the Common are considered to be the earthworks which date from the Iron Age. It has been suggested by certain historians that the whole complex of mounds and ditches at Minchinhampton is far more important than is appreciated by the average resident of today's town, for this could have been a huge base camp or

*Left: The Crown Inn*

*Right: Tom Long's Post, Minchinhampton Common*

*Below: At the bottom of Minchinhampton's High Street*

*Left:* *Across the Common at Minchinhampton*
*Below:* *Former mill buildings in the Golden Valley, below Minchinhampton*

safe area for those of the Dobunni tribes who opposed the Romans. After the initial fighting in which the invaders defeated the native tribesmen, the leader of the Dobunni, known as Caractacus, escaped. Some years later he became the leader of those who resisted in the mountainous terrain of Wales. Possibly during the interim period he could well have spent his time here at Minchinhampton gathering his followers and preparing them for opposition to the Romans and those who had befriended them. The plateau of Minchinhampton is fairly high at around 600ft and with a steep escarpment as a natural defence together with the addition of ramparts and ditches the whole area could well have become a massive and easily defendable encampment. To the west of today's town are the most impressive of these bold pieces of ancient architecture. The Bulwarks, as they have become known, curve to the southeast and were excavated about 60 years ago when a ditch measuring up to 7m wide and 2m deep cut out of solid rock was uncovered. The rubble from the ditch had been used to construct a huge bank about 2m high x 10m wide which was retained by a drystone wall. A further ditch of similar dimensions but only 70m long points out almost as a finger toward Amberly.

Numerous "pillow mounds" will also be observed by the visitor to Minchinhampton Common; these usually measure about 16m x 3m x 0.5m. It is thought that these were man made rabbit warrens; one is situated between the reservoir and the golf house.

Amongst the evidence of early man in the vicinity of Minchinhampton is Whitfield's Tump. Today it takes the form of a grassy mound about 1m x 25m x 10m and dates from about 2,500 BC. Originally it was constructed as a large burial mound and in 1743 George Whitfield used it as his pulpit when he preached to a large congregation on the Common, hence its name. It has been estimated that 40 burials could have been housed within an inner stone chamber. At the east end of the mound a deep hollow indicates that it could have been excavated at some time during history, possibly by grave robbers, but there is no proof of this. Further a metal seat marks the spot known as Jacob's Knoll, a mound which is circular in shape and was formerly a round barrow. It is estimated that this one dates from between 2,000 - 700 BC.

The visitor to Minchinhampton will no doubt wish to explore the Common but should be aware that it is for the most part to be shared with the golfer. The Minchinhampton Golf Club dates back to 1889 and these enthusiastic players must surely enjoy one of the finest and historically connected courses in southern England.

Following the Norman conquest the Manor of Minchinhampton was "acquired" by the new rulers and passed to L'Abbaye aux Dames' which was the Convent of the Holy Trinity at Caen. The Lady of the Manor was then the Abbess who received the revenues from this new estate while her affairs were conducted on her behalf by her representatives here while she remained at Caen. Around 1213 she purchased for Minchinhampton the right to hold weekly markets; this of course added to her revenues while giving town status to Minchinhampton. By 1424 Syon Abbey had inherited the manor as during the reign of Henry IV properties which belonged to foreign ecclesiastical orders were taken by the crown and redistributed.

When Henry VIII dissolved the monasteries the manor was passed to the 1st. Baron Windsor whose family sold it in 1656 to Samuel Sheppard. His family retained it until 1814. The Ricardo's were the next lords of the Manor and residing at Gatcombe they remained until 1913. The National Trust then purchased the Common from the Ricardo's, thus the line of Lordship of the Manor of Minchinhampton drew to a close.

The famous house Gatcombe Park was constructed for the Sheppards, one of the wealthy clothiers of Minchinhampton in the 1770s. By 1947 it was owned by Rab Butler, the late Lord Butler of Saffron Walden, and as most people know is currently the home of the Princess Royal and Commander Timothy Lawrence.

**MINCHINHAMPTON**

| | |
|---|---|
| P | Parking |
| P.O. | Post Office |
| T | Toilets |
| 1 | Church of the Holy Trinity |
| 2 | The Market House |
| 3 | Crown Inn |
| 4 | Arden House and Cottage |
| 5 | The former White Hart Inn |
| 6 | Building dated 1682 |

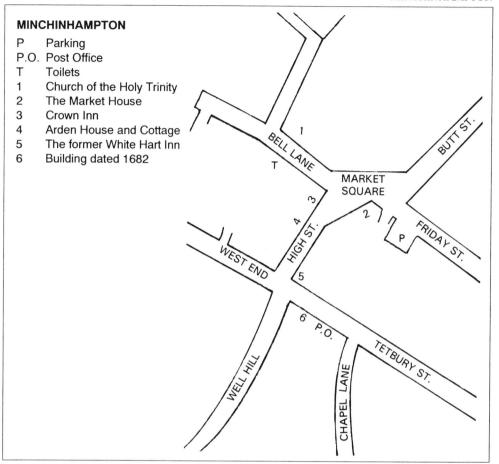

*Above: Minchinhampton's Market House dates from 1698*
*Below: The impressive architecture of Minchinhampton's High Street*

# 13: Moreton-in-Marsh

It is well known that the Romans built their roads in straight lines, thus at Moreton the main street is as straight as a die, just as the Romans left it. The only exception is the positioning of the Redesdale Hall which makes a pleasant break to the otherwise geometric lines of the shops, inns and cottages that line the Fosse Way.

The unusual name of Moreton-in-Marsh came, in part at least, from the Saxons. Moreton meant 'Farmstead on the moor' and during the Saxon period that is what it was, a farming community set in a rather bleak landscape. Much later 'In Marsh' was added. This may have been a reference to the boggy land along the banks of the River Evenlode, but this is only one of a number of possible explanations.

As a result of archaeological evidence human settlements in the locality are known to have existed during the Bronze Age. 700 years later a Roman fortification is thought to have been built close to where the town's cricket ground is today, when it was probably used to subdue the people of the Dobunni tribe who inhabited various parts of the Cotswolds. Later, during the 9th century Moreton was passed by its Saxon lord to the monastery of Deerhurst which

*The Old Fosse Way, Memorial and the Bell Inn*

*The Old Curfew Tower*

*The Manor House Hotel and the Fosse Way*

lies to the west, close by the River Severn. A century later, however, its estates were confiscated by the Mercians and passed into the possession of Earl Odda, whose tiny chapel, only discovered in 1885, still stands at Deerhurst. Later Moreton became the property of the wife of Edward the Confessor and in turn via the King to the newer abbey at Westminster.

During the early years of the 13th century the Abbey's Abbot, Richard of Barking, decided that Moreton should be given the opportunity to develop just as the other nearby towns of Campden and Stowe had done. To this end he pressed Henry III for a charter granting permission for a weekly market to be held and he instigated the development of a 'new' town with its wide main street astride the Fosse Way.

By 1387 Richard II was at odds with his barons and the areas close to Moreton were threatened. The Earl of Oxford, loyal to the King, was en route from the city of Chester with an army of 4,000 men to join the King at Windsor. The Duke of Gloucester having taken the surrounding hamlets assembled his troops at Moreton in readiness for the ensuing action, only to be evaded by the Earl of Oxford. For a while peace returned and the people of Moreton

went back to farming the land and grazing sheep.

Following Henry VIII's Dissolution of the Monasteries, Moreton had a number of different 'owners', eventually the Lordship of the Manor of Bourton-on-the-Hill and Moreton being gained once more by the dean and chapter of Westminster. During later centuries large parcels of land in and around the town were purchased by the Creswick family, while the Manor, still owned by Westminster Abbey until 1856, was bought complete by the Redesdale family.

Toward the end of the 18th century the poor in this part of England endured considerable hardship for a series of bad harvests had reduced them to near starvation. The upper class were little affected by this and continued to enjoy a good lifestyle. During this time the Creswick estate known as Sezincote was bought by Sir Charles Cockerell in 1795. A colonel in the service of the East India Company, he died three years later, the estate being inherited by his younger brothers. The large house which was built between them no doubt reflected the family's strong connections with India. Its mock Indian grandeur and unusual combination of architectural styles greatly

influenced the Prince Regent and his ideas for the famous Brighton Pavilion just a few years later.

As with many of the Cotswold towns, the days of coach travel were busy indeed for Moreton. Straddling the Fosse Way it became a natural coaching town on the routes between Worcester, Stratford, Oxford and beyond. The arrival of the railways, whilst putting an end to the coach travel trade with all its ancillary businesses, did much to stimulate the town's development. Consequently much of the town's architecture, with only a few exceptions, dates from this period in the early 1800s.

*Wagon of the Stratford to Moreton Railway*

For Moreton the railway age began a little earlier than for most other places for here on 28th May 1821 an Act of Parliament brought into being the Stratford and Moreton Railway Company, just six weeks after the opening of the Stockton to Darlington Railway. However the railway between Stratford on Avon and Moreton-in-Marsh was in fact a horse powered tramway. It was decided, perhaps short sightedly, to use a well proven power source, i.e. the horse, rather than the steam engine, which had at that time been functioning for only a short period of time and was not proven. The aim of the Stratford and Moreton Railway Company was to provide a more direct and therefore more economical means of transport, primarily for coal, from Stratford on Avon to Moreton-in-Marsh.

On completion of the Stratford Canal in 1816 the transport from the Midlands to Stratford on Avon was made more direct than in the past and it was felt that a direct route from the termination basin of the canal to Moreton-in-Marsh should be made by way of the tramway. William James of Henley in Arden, who was to have much to do with the initial planning of the Liverpool and Manchester Railway, was prominent in the early development of the tramway venture. He was a colliery owner and was involved in the concept of a canal to link Stratford and Abingdon to the River Thames. He also had further imaginative notions for the Moreton tramway. Indeed there were certain parties who were planning to include the tramway from Stratford to Moreton within a much more imaginative undertaking, a tramway system which would link the whole of the industrial midlands with London.

With hindsight it is easy to condemn the decisions made more than a century and a half ago. It is now clear to see that at the

*Below: The Old Parsonage*
*Right: St David's Church*

time the future development of a transport system lay not with horse power applied as it was to canal barge or to rail tram but to steam power; until such time of course as the internal combustion engine rendered steam obsolete! The Stratford and Moreton Tramway therefore did not last long for within thirty years of its opening parts of the line were closed and on other parts the steam locomotive had taken over.

Sadly little evidence of this venture exists today. At Moreton-in-Marsh near the Railway Station the site where the old tramway terminus and stable buildings once stood is now home to a supermarket

and at the old railway's northern terminus in Stratford on Avon a solitary waggon is all that remains of the railway's rolling stock.

By 1861 the section of the railway line between Hereford and Worcester was linked with the Oxford, Worcester and Wolverhampton Railway which ran through Moreton. Before long this in turn became part of the Great Western Railway network thus ensuring the town's rail links well into the 20th century.

During the late 1800s Batsford Park was built to the north of the town by Lord Redesdale. A simple and traditional building, the front entrance faces north. It

has a porch which projects from its centre between two wings, the right one of which contains a ballroom. At the rear, the garden front faces south and has three projecting bays beneath pointed gables; while from the roof a host of tall chimneys point skyward. This handsome building in local stone is set amidst its now famous gardens and Arboretum.

Back in Moreton's High Street is further evidence of the town's close connection with the Redesdale family. The well known and quite handsome Town Hall was built for the Redesdale's as Redesdale Hall by Sir Ernest George in 1887. It stands, like so

many of the much earlier Cotswold guildhalls, raised on open arches. On its high pointed roof is a clock tower topped by a boar's head weathervane which is supported by a series of interwoven arches. A tall chimney rises from the wall which faces the High Street and the family crest of the Redesdale's is embossed in stone on its southern wall. This building may have been constructed on the site of a much earlier market hall, references to which were made during the 18th century.

The oldest building in the town, the Curfew Tower dating from the 16th century, whilst having an inscription of

*Left:*    *The Old School, Moreton-in-Marsh*
*Right:*   *The Four Shire Stone near Moreton-in-Marsh*

1782, faces the Redesdale Hall across the busy High Street from the corner of Oxford Street. It is topped by a gabled turret, a clock dated 1648 and a bell of 1633. It seems that a curfew bell was rung here from as early as the 11th century when it would have indicated to the citizens that it was time to dowse their fires and retire for the night; the bell still rang the curfew until 1860 and during later years it was used to summon the fire brigade. On the tower wall at a readable height is a hand lettered notice giving the market tolls. It is dated 1905.

At the southern end of the High Street where it is joined by Church Street is one of the town's best known buildings. The much modified Manor House Hotel, dated 1658, is claimed by some to be the most haunted hotel in town. Formerly it was Creswyke House and was not used as a hotel until the Second World War. In 1752 the property was bought by Benjamin Busby, a linen weaver, for a bargain price because it was believed to be haunted. The Dame Creswyke was, it seems, murdered in the house and it is she who is reputed to appear from time to time, the most recent appearance according to records being in 1987.

Throughout the 18th century the nearby land provided Moreton with a ready supply of flax resulting in work for about forty weavers within the town itself, with further work being carried out on cottage looms in local hamlets. By the early years of the 19th century the cultivation of flax was almost over but the weaving continued for a considerable time after.

The town's Church of St. David, built in 1848 with various additions to its structure until 1890, is situated behind the High Street and was originally a chapel-of-ease for nearby Bourton-on-the-Hill. The immediate area surrounding the church is where the town's original settlement was before the development along the Fosse Way. To the

west of the church is the Old Parsonage dating from the early 19th century. In a terrace of houses to the east of the church of St. Davids is an 18th century house of two storeys with dormer windows, while Lilac Cottage with its stone mullioned windows is about 100 years older.

Back on the High Street the town is well endowed with old coaching inns and hotels. In addition to the already mentioned Manor House Hotel is the former 17th century Manor House, now the White Hart Royal Hotel, where it is claimed Charles I stayed on 2nd July 1644. Almost opposite is the Redesdale Arms built in the late 18th century. Before 1891 it was known as the Unicorn. While the town's main asset is its broad High Street lined with stone buildings of shops and houses, Oxford Street is also interesting. Beyond the Curfew Tower and on an 'island' is the Mann Institute. Built of rusticated stone and with a timber framed gable end it dates from 1891. The inscription reads, 'Every noble life leaves the fibre of it interwoven for ever in the Work of the World'. On the north side is the Congregational Church of 1860 and a little further on before the road crosses the railway line is the attractive building of the Infant School. It was built in 1851 (the same year as the Great Exhibition) and has three storeys. Close by is the large Leamington House with its gable and chimney of the 16th century.

Unlike the neighbouring town of Stow-on-the-Wold, Moreton never enjoyed the prosperity during medieval times that came from the wool trade, consequently it has little of architectural merit from this period, though its Tuesday market, which causes certain traffic problems today, is a good reminder of a very old tradition.

Outside Moreton and alongside the road to Chipping Norton (A44) is another leftover from the past. The Four Shires Stone formerly marked the boundaries

between the counties of Worcestershire, Gloucestershire, Oxfordshire and Warwickshire. The boundaries that meet here are now only three. The newer county of Hereford and Worcester is in fact about ten miles away.

**MORETON-IN-MARSH**

| | |
|---|---|
| P | Parking |
| P.O. | Post Office |
| T | Toilets |
| 1 | Church of St. David |
| 2 | The Old Parsonage |
| 3 | Manor House Hotel |
| 4 | The Old Corn Exchange |
| 5 | The White Hart Royal Hotel |
| 6 | The Redesdale Arms |
| 7 | The Redesdale Hall |
| 8 | The Curfew Tower |
| 9 | The Mann Institute |
| 10 | Railway Station |

# 14: Painswick

At the western edge of the Cotswolds, where the stonework of its medieval buildings lose their tinge of honey in exchange for the pale grey, stands the attractive town of Painswick. Unspoilt over recent years Painswick has managed to retain much of the atmosphere of the days gone by when its income came from the weaving of cloth. Unlike other Cotswold towns Painswick seems to be without a centre; instead it consists of a beautiful conglomeration of side streets each containing buildings of historical and architectural interest.

In Vicarage Street there stands the 17th century Yew Tree House, home of the clothier Thomas Loveday. In Bisley Street the former 14th century Fleece Inn is now divided into two properties called Wickstone and Little Fleece, owned by the National Trust. Adjacent to Wickstone and also dating from the 14th century, Chur has an arched doorway that was built to facilitate the entrance of donkeys carrying packs of fleece. New Street contains four interesting buildings - the 17th century Packers and Hazelbury House, the 18th century Falcon Hotel, formerly used for cock fighting, and the 15th century Post Office. The timber framed front of the Post

*The Oldest Post Office in England*

*Wickstone in Bisley Street at Painswick*

89

Office is the last surviving example of its type in Painswick. The original name for the building was Westhaven House and it was probably owned by a rich merchant.

Down by the river, the Painswick Stream, is Savoury's Pin Mill which was still used until the early 19th century for the production of cloth. Since then it has been used as a corn mill, then for the production of pins, paper clips and the like until 1983 when it was sold for conversion into a private home. A similar fate has befallen the other former mills along the stream.

The remains of the defence ramparts built by the original inhabitants of the region are still visible today on Painswick Beacon. Within the safety of the ramparts a settlement of wattle, mud and timber dwellings was developed and the residents lived by a combination of herding cattle, hunting and agriculture long before the Romans arrived at Cirencester and Gloucester.

For about 350 years after the Romans conquered the region they ruled until the Saxons invaded and swarmed over the rich landscape of Gloucestershire as it is now. A small band of the new conquerors cleared the thickly forested area where St. Mary's Church stands today. They constructed their own village and later a church, thus Painswick was founded.

Hundreds of years later during the early 11th century Edward the Confessor was handing out most of the prestigious and important positions in this part of England to his Norman colleagues but Earl Godwin of the Saxons was very opposed to this practice. He, with his followers of Wessex freemen, were said to have threatened the King from the top of Painswick Beacon, consequently the name of Godwin has continued to be associated with the town ever since. Nevertheless this manor, amongst others, was given by the King to Walter de Lacy, no doubt as a reward for his support at Hastings. By 1085 when Domesday was compiled, "Wicke", for it was still known by its Saxon name, had a male population of 70 persons which included a priest and it is thought that about this time no less than four flour mills were operating along the Wick Stream.

The name of Painswick, often like so many other towns and villages of England, dates from this period in our history or even earlier. Painswick is usually ascribed to Pain Fitzjohn, who was not one of the original Norman conquerors but one of the next generation of Normans who had been

*Left:* St Mary's, Painswick
*Below:* Table top tombs amidst the 99 clipped yew trees in the graveyard of St Mary's

born here in England. He was also the Sheriff to Henry I. Thus by a combination of his name and the old Saxon name Wicke, the place became known as Pain's Wicke and later Painswick.

Unfortunately by 1137 Pain had lost his life, having become a victim of a Welsh archer during a skirmish with the wild Welsh. The manor then passed to his son-in-law who, when Pain's daughter failed to produce a child, left her to become a monk at Llanthory Abbey, Gloucester. Pain's youngest daughter, however, fared better through her marriage to Warine de Munchensi and as a result of their union the manor of Painswick progressed steadily under the direction of Munchensi descendants who became enthusiastic farmers, working much of the lands in the surrounding villages and hamlets. The third of the Munchensi descendants to hold the manor was a great mediator who continually strove for a peaceful settlement to the disputes between Simon de Montfort, the Earl of Leicester and King Henry III. However other members of the Munchensi family began to sympathize with Simon de Montfort and with their troops captured Henry III and his son Edward at Lewes in 1264.

A year later Prince Edward escaped and with the backing of the English lords of the Welsh border country, forced the Earl Simon to retreat to Evesham. At Kenilworth reinforcements were close to hard pressed de Montford but during the night Prince Edward and his army fell upon them. The following day they disposed of the Earl Simon and his followers who were trapped in a loop of the River Avon.

The sons of the Munchensi's and the de Montfords, William and Simon respectively, escaped to Kenilworth Castle and as they were on the losing side they had forfeited their manors. In spite of repeated attempts to storm the castle they held out for eight months, repelling each attack until eventually the attackers relented and on a promise to conform to the King's will their manors and estates were restored to them. William of the Munchensi's died 20 years later fighting for Edward I in the Black Mountains against the Welsh.

During the mid 1300s the name of the Despensers features prominently in certain events. Hugh Despenser was without doubt one of the favourites of Edward II and a powerful man of dubious character. One story tells of Elizabeth who was the rightful heiress to the Manor of Painswick being abducted by Hugh Despenser and his henchmen and tortured until she agreed to hand over to him the Painswick manor. The fairy tale ending to the story is that she was rescued by the dashing young hero Sir Richard Talbot, who of course carried her away and married her. About that time all of England was rising up against the King and his repeated choice of favourites. Hugh Despenser was pursued and eventually captured at Bristol where he was hung without a trial while Edward II was imprisoned in the Berkeley Castle where he was later murdered.

Of all the families associated with Painswick throughout history one of the best thought of was the Talbots. John Talbot, Earl of Shrewsbury, was reputed to have fought many battles against the French, some say as many as forty. In the local villages he became known as 'King Talbot' for his continual opposition to Joan of Arc and he was noted for his fair dealings towards the commoners. He made certain concessions to tenant farmers, allowing them the free use of timber growing on their land. He allowed widowers of commoners to use their former husbands' common land grazing rights even if they remarried and he let out to tenants certain of his own lands which he had formerly farmed himself. At Lodge Farm in nearby Sheepscombe the

*Painswick's side streets give way to fine views*

former hunting lodge of the Talbot family still stands today.

John Talbot had two wives. His second was the Lady Margaret who claimed that she and not her cousin Lord Berkeley was the rightful owner of the nearby Berkeley estates together with the notorious castle. This claim was to cause much trouble in Painswick and the neighbouring countryside as each family retaliated against the other. A summons on John Berkeley was delivered by David Woodburne on behalf of the Talbots but the summons written on parchment and sealed with wax was stuffed into the mouth of the

unfortunate Mr Woodburne. The angry Berkeleys sent a raiding party to plunder the town of Painswick and in return the son of the Talbots put the town of Berkeley to the torch. Following the collection of the Talbots' rents the monies had been stored beneath the floorboards at the home of Richard Andrews. This snippet of information found its way to the Berkeleys whereupon a further raiding party was sent out at night to take the prize. After turning the house upside down and threatening the owner they discovered a chest filled with the Talbots' rents. Unfortunately for Berkeley's men the Talbots had got wind of

this latest move against them, or maybe they had leaked the information deliberately, for a troop of Talbot horsemen had surrounded the house and when the Berkeleys attempted to make their getaway they were taken prisoner. As they arrived at Berkeley Castle in the darkness Rice Tewe, the Berkeleys' leader, under the threat of death called for the drawbridge to be lowered and the Talbots together with their hostages entered the castle. Lord Berkeley and his four sons were arrested by the Talbots and family feuding was finished for a time. Sadly John Talbot and his son Viscount Lisle were to die side by side in

1452 at Castillon while fighting the French. They were fighting in support of the men of Gascony who rose against the King of France in order to regain their former allegiance to the English throne. The manor of Painswick then passed to Thomas Talbot, the grandson of John.

By 1496 the 63 year old Lord Berkeley married Joan Talbot, John's daughter by his first marriage. This resulted in him being able to claim back his lands and Berkeley Castle and once again there was friction between the two families. The impetuous young Thomas then challenged the Berkeleys to settle their differences by the

*Right: Up the hill to the 'Golden Heart'*
*Below: Loveday's house*

sword and the battle that followed at nearby Nibly Green was the last in England to be fought by private armies. Thomas was killed and the discovery of a communal grave during recent centuries indicates that about 150 men of both sides also lost their lives. This battle resulted in the end of the Talbots' power and prestige at Painswick as Thomas Talbot's sister moved with her daughter to the family hunting lodge at Sheepscombe.

Almost a hundred years later the manor of Painswick was sold to Thomas Cromwell, a minister of Henry VIII, but when he was beheaded the King made a present of the manor to Sir Anthony Kingston, a Provost Marshall of the Crown, who incidentally escorted Bishop Hooper through the streets of Gloucester on his last journey, to be burned at the stake beside the great Cathedral. Later, after the death of Henry VIII he returned to Painswick where he plotted to raise an army to replace Queen Mary with Elizabeth I. He was arrested but was drowned in the Thames at Lechlade while trying to escape from his captors who were transporting him to London. From then until as recently as 1804 the Manor of Painswick was held by the Jerningham family.

During the Civil War, while nearby Gloucester had declared itself to be a Cromwellian city, tiny Painswick was a Royalist town. At that time Sir Ralph Dutton, who had leased Painswick's manorial rights from the Jerningham family, led the assault against the Roundheads at Bristol in 1643. With the fall of Bristol the King turned his attention to Gloucester and having travelled by way of Berkeley and Cirencester arrived in Painswick on 9th August to be joined by Prince Rupert who had stayed close by at Prinknash. As the reader will now be aware the siege of Gloucester was a disaster for the King, after

*Left:*   *Down the narrow streets of Painswick*
*Right:*  *Former mills in the Slad Valley near Painswick*

*Left:* The tiny 'Woolpack Inn' at Slad
*Below:* The Slad Valley near Painswick

which he marched on to Newbury. Meanwhile the Roundheads attacked Painswick but withdrew, leaving many dead and wounded behind. Soon the Royalist forces were required elsewhere and the Cromwellians regained control for a time occupying the church and a number of houses in the town. Sir William Varasaur was given the task of clearing the invaders from the town and church. The scars of this battle are still visible in places on the outside of St. Mary's. The Roundheads were cleared but later the same year, December 1644, they returned and as the Royalist cause was waning they replaced the vicar and his family with their own Puritan Mr Dorwood. Sir Ralph Dutton continued to fight for the King's cause until, almost at the eleventh hour, he was shipwrecked and drowned as he escaped to France.

One of the many mysteries associated with the English Civil War is worth mentioning here as it concerns Painswick and the building known as the Fiery Beacon Gallery. Today's building was extended at the front during the 18th century so that the outer wall that existed during those troubled times is now an inner wall. At the time when the Parliamentarians had barricaded themselves in the church the King's troops assembled here to light their torches before making an assault on St. Mary's. From time to time since then there have been a number of sightings of a light within the building. As recently as 1984 an overseas visitor who had photographed the building without a flash was amazed, after having the resultant photograph developed, to see a flame burning on the wall. A study of the photograph failed to reveal that it had in any way been interfered with but the building's owner cannot give an explanation as she has not experienced this strange phenomenon.

A church at Painswick was mentioned in the Domesday Book but since then the church has gradually been rebuilt. The north aisle was constructed during the late 1300s but rebuilt in 1480 in the English Perpendicular style, with two corbels representing Richard II and his Queen. Within the small chapel of the lords of the manor which is dedicated to St. Peter is a large tomb of Purbeck marble. This was originally a tomb of the Talbot family but later became the tomb of the Kingstons and beneath it Henry VIII's Governor of the Tower of London lies buried. Strangely, the effigies of Dr. Seaman and his wife were taken from the Chancel and added to this 'two family' tomb in 1743.

The whole of this small chapel was rebuilt at the same period as the north aisle, the central nave and the tower but the steeple was added some 150 years later. The south aisle was added in 1741, its Gothic arcade dating from the late 17th century.

If St. Mary's is the best known building to the visitors to Painswick it is not due to its antiquity for many other Cotswold churches are much older, but mainly to its unusual churchyard with its 99 yew trees and endless table top tombs of the 17th and 18th centuries.

Only a short distance from Painswick and enjoying its magnificent hillside setting is Prinknash Abbey. Unusually modern in appearance but with an unusual history it is worth mentioning here.

Only five years after the Abbot of Gloucester had hosted Henry VIII and Anne Boleyn at the manor of Prinknash, the Dissolution of the Monasteries meant that in 1540 the whole estate like so many others was surrendered to the Crown. From then on it passed into the hands of many owners until as recently as 1928 when it again became the property of the Benedictine order of monks, the original owners almost 400 years earlier.

Four years after the Dissolution Sir Anthony Kingston, the then owner, died and Henry VIII made a present of it to Lord Chandos of Sudeley who was the owner of Sudeley Castle at Winchcombe. By 1628 the Prinknash estate had been purchased by Sir John Bridgeman who restored the medieval chapel and whose widow still lived at Prinknash throughout the Civil War. After the Civil War it passed to a number of different owners until in more recent years its owner was Thomas Dyer Edwards who did much to modify the parkland and the house itself. The most significant thing as far as today's Abbey is concerned is that in 1924 only two years before his death, he

became a Catholic. On his death his grandson honoured his wishes and granted the whole of Prinknash Park to the Benedictine order.

Before the Second World War the monks had outgrown the old house at Prinknash and had planned to build anew but the new building was not completed until 1972. Today's building is not to everyone's taste, in fact to many it appears to be rather stark and forbidding in its appearance, but it is modern and functional, divorced from luxury and ostentation.

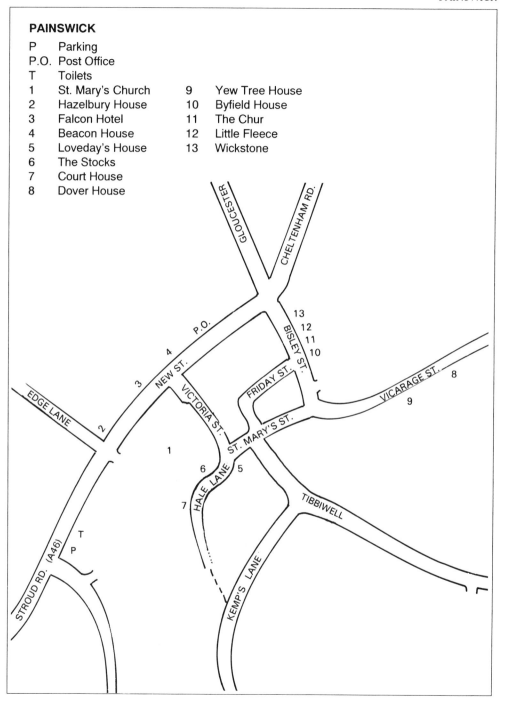

**PAINSWICK**

P    Parking
P.O.  Post Office
T    Toilets
1    St. Mary's Church          9    Yew Tree House
2    Hazelbury House           10   Byfield House
3    Falcon Hotel              11   The Chur
4    Beacon House              12   Little Fleece
5    Loveday's House           13   Wickstone
6    The Stocks
7    Court House
8    Dover House

# 15: Stow-on-the-Wold

*The architecture of the Market Square*

Across the top of the nearby hills and along the ancient tracks came the very early hunters, many of them coming from across the River Severn while others, the Beaker people, came from the Thames valley. At first they came in search of prey and later to barter for wool with iron products. Their offspring settled the land and intermarried with the natives of the surrounding areas. Later came the Romans, clearing, building and developing their roadways but Stow's development owes much to its position as do many of our old towns and villages.

Stow sat at the place where the ancient Ridgeway met the Roman Fosse Way, at a hub in fact of the old trade routes high above the hills. Its height is a mere 700ft above sea level, not really high at all, but nevertheless it is the highest town in the Cotswolds. Like so many of the other Cotswold towns its prosperity came from wool and throughout the medieval period it continued to develop and expand.

During later generations Stow was to experience much turbulence as the storm clouds gathered pre-empting the English Civil War. Due to its position on high ground, the town was to become familiar with the sight, sound and smell of war. After the declaration of war in 1642, the King chose to make his capital at Oxford from where the Royalist strategy was to control the whole of Gloucester and the west Midlands. This in turn meant that the control of the castles of Berkeley and Sudeley together with control of all the influential country houses became increasingly important in order to achieve this objective. During the ensuing years the King was to visit Stow on two occasions, first in 1644 and a year later when he was escorted by 1,000 horse and foot soldiers. It was then that he proclaimed the best inn between Worcester and London was the King's Arms at Stow.

During March of the following year Sir Jacob Astley, Governor of Worcester was ordered by the King to proceed with his troops to Oxford. Unfortunately for the Royalists these plans found their way into the hands of the Parliamentarians who closed in on them from all sides and by 21st March 1646 the two armies faced each other at Donnington just outside Stow. The Royalists were outnumbered and after desperate fighting retreated into the town itself where, it was recorded later, Digbeth Street was awash with blood as Englishman fought Englishman.

The ageing Astley surrendered and with

200 of his troops dead the remaining 1,600 prisoners were packed into the Church of St. Edward, just behind the town square, as this was the only secure building able to accommodate such a number. Thus, due Astley's failure to reach the King at Oxford, the King surrendered and the war was over, for a while at least.

Five years later, the King having escaped and been recaptured was imprisoned at Carisbrooke Castle and eventually was executed. His eldest son then reassembled with his supporters and was in turn defeated at the battle of Worcester in 1651 and passed once again through the Cotswolds in his attempt to escape to France. He and his associates were naturally pursued by the troops of the New Model Army who, while failing to catch up with him, did succeed in catching up with Arthur Jones of Chastleton House, just a few miles from Stow, whom they mistakenly believed to be the King. According to one story his pursuers, failing to find him, spent the night in the very room behind the panels of which their quarry was hiding. Fortunately for Arthur Jones, his wife Sarah drugged the Cromwellians with laudanum whilst her husband made good his escape.

*Above*
*Left:* The old stocks
*Right:* Church Street from the gate of St Edward's Church

*Left:* The Battle of Stow Memorial, St Edward's churchyard
*Right:* St Edward's Church

The Chastleton estate was at one point owned by Robert Catesby who, as most people will remember from their school days, was one of the members of the Gunpowder Plot conspiracy. He eventually sold it for £4,000 to Walter Jones who was a wealthy wool stapler, in order to raise funds to pay for his part in the Essex rebellion. The large, imposing Jacobean house was built around 1603 and since then it has undergone no major alteration. Regarded by many as one of the most notable of Britain's country houses of its period Chastleton was on the market in 1991 for the first time since it was sold by Robert

Catesby. It is now owned by the National Trust and has been opened to a small number of visitors since 1996.

Today's Stow is certainly a pleasant and popular town. During its earlier years it was named by the Abbot of Evesham as Stowe St Edward, the name was retained until the 16th century when it became known as Stow-on-the-Wold. Busy all the year round with a steady flow of visitors, Stow has been an important market town since medieval times.

It has always been a traditional centre for sheep and horse fairs and at its height was reputed, by Daniel Defoe, to have seen

the sale of 20,000 animals a day taking place. Even today the horse fair is still held twice yearly in a field just out of the town centre and it is probably one of the largest events of its kind in the country. Many years ago the fair was held in the market square but with the gradual encroachment of the buildings as the town developed this became impractical.

As the visitor approaches the town the tower of St Edward's Church dominates the landscape for many a mile due to its high vantage point to the west of the square. In AD986 Earl Aethelmer, Duke of Cornwall was attributed with the building of a church

*Below: The Market Square*
*Right: Early morning at Stow*

98

at Stow. No remains of this are visible today, nor is much left of the later 12th century Norman church except for a flat buttress on the outer wall below the west window at the end of the nave. However with the development of the town's fortunes from the wool trade a great deal of money was donated to the church. This resulted in the alteration and expansion of the building from the 13th to the 15th centuries and consequently there are various architectural styles in evidence today. The handsome Perpendicular tower which took two years to build was completed in 1447. It stands 88ft high on walls up to 6ft thick and is topped with battlements and gargoyles.

After the Civil War the church was declared a ruin until restoration work commenced on it in 1700. Further restoration was carried out, though thankfully in a quite tasteful manner, during the reign of Queen Victoria. Just as the rich wool staplers of the Cotswolds had done hundreds of years earlier the rich Victorians put money into their churches, in some cases rebuilding them completely. The Gothic style was dominant in ecclesiastical architecture at this time and most of the stained glass in our churches which had been damaged during the Reformation and later during the Civil War was replaced by the enthusiastic and well meaning Victorians. Fortunately St. Edward's still retains some earlier items of interest. The most recent is probably the Baroque memorial of 1668 on the chancel wall dedicated to the Chamberlyne family. They were the manorial lords of Stowe and nearby Maugersbury and were great benefactors to the church. A little older is the crucifiction painting in the south aisle, claimed to be by Gasper de Craeyer who was a contemporary of Van Dyck and of Rubens. Perhaps the most fitting item is the tomb of the unfortunate Captain Keyte, one of the Royalists who died in the heavy fighting of the Civil War. Visitors are able to enjoy the church in its quiet position which is almost like an enclosed back garden of the buildings that front onto the hustle and bustle of the town's square.

St. Edward's Hall of 1878 stands solid and Gothic at the centre of the Square. It was erected at a cost of £4,000, the sum being provided by unclaimed deposits in the Town Savings Bank. Earlier in the century the Provident Bank had been founded in the Square in order to encourage the residents to become thrifty people. In 1861 the Post Office Savings Bank opened

*Digbeth Street*

*Clouds over Stow Town Hall*

and the Provident then transferred its business to the newcomer. A substantial amount was unclaimed and this was duly invested gaining interest. Having advertised for the claimants to come forward to collect their gains the trustees eventually gave the money to pay for the hall. Close inspection of the stonework on each side of the front door reveals rope niches which were caused by horse users treating the stonework in the same way as the cowboys in the Westerns used the hitching rails. Above the door is a figure of St. Edward and above that again is the steeple which was added in 1895 to

*The Royalist Hotel*

accommodate the bell used to summon the volunteer fire fighters.

The Square nowadays is a large car parking area but at its northern end is a small sanctuary of lawn known as The Green. Earlier this century before the intrusion of the family car The Green was much larger and was often used for sheep grazing. On The Green are the most recent of Stowe's stocks which date from the 15th century. They were moved here during the building of St. Edward's Hall.

At the southern end of the Square is the Market Cross. It was erected early in the 12th century as a symbolic reminder to medieval traders to deal honestly in the market place and to carry out their business transactions in a Christian manner. In 1878 the gabled headstone was added and at one time illumination was provided by a gas lamp.

Facing the Cross is the Talbot Hotel, built in 1714 and one of the many interesting buildings that surround the Square. The Talbot was formerly the Corn Exchange where samples of corn were brought for valuation. The existing letter box in the hotel wall is thought to be the place through which the samples were posted. To the left is one of a number of narrow alleys which give access to the Square. These were designed so that the animals, primarily sheep, could be counted as they entered the sales area. Just up Church Street is the old St. Edward's Grammar School. The school was founded in 1475, rebuilt with rubble masonry with stone mullioned windows during the late 16th century and is today the Masonic Hall.

The buildings mainly fronted by shops on the west side of the Square provide the visitors with architecture of different periods and styles. The most decorative façade is that of the St. Edward's Cafe with its entrance steps leading to an arched doorway above which is an arched niche. The building is three storeys high and is greatly enhanced by its fluted Corinthian pilasters to either side. Further along, the lopsided building of 1450 seems to defy all the laws of perspective, but its foundations rest on bastions, probably installed to support an older house of 'cruck' construction.

On the opposite side of the Square the Youth Hostel stands proud as a beacon to young travellers of all denominations while

*St Edward's Café*

close by is Ross House, formerly the Plough. The King's Arms is situated on the left just before Digbeth Street and is a fine example of an old Cotswold coaching inn. The granting of the inn's licence is said to have been by Edward VI in 1548. The truth is a matter of conjecture but the inn certainly existed by the mid 1600s. At one time it was a posting house with its main entrance by way of the arch which led to the rear stables. Alterations have moved the entrance during more recent years but the coat of arms of Henry VIII can still be seen on the wall.

On the left in Digbeth Street is an old house, now business premises, which has a fine arched doorway and old stone mullioned windows. Most of the buildings in this narrow street are of 16th and 17th century origins with more modern shop fronts. Further down on the left is one of the town's most famous hotels. The Royalist Hotel features in the *Guinness Book of Records* and is claimed to be the oldest in England; there are however a number of other claimants to the title. The original building is oak framed and is thought to date from the 10th century, its front façade being added in 1615. During the 13th and 15th centuries the building was known as the Eagle and Child and at one time it served as a hospice for the old, the sick and the poor of the town. As is frequently the case the final claim of a house of this stature is the tunnel or secret passage. This one, it is said, connects with the manor at close by Maugersbury. Further, the ghost of a woman is said to appear from time to time in the upper corridors, the last sighting being during the 1970s.

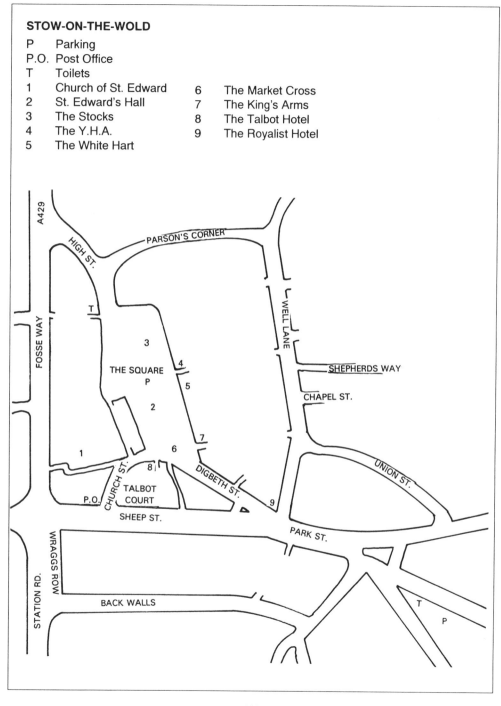

**STOW-ON-THE-WOLD**

P    Parking
P.O.  Post Office
T    Toilets

| | | | |
|---|---|---|---|
| 1 | Church of St. Edward | 6 | The Market Cross |
| 2 | St. Edward's Hall | 7 | The King's Arms |
| 3 | The Stocks | 8 | The Talbot Hotel |
| 4 | The Y.H.A. | 9 | The Royalist Hotel |
| 5 | The White Hart | | |

# 16: Tetbury

In 1971 the small, stone hill town of Tetbury was designated as an outstanding conservation area and rightly so! It has all the ingredients that should be treated with respect and preserved for future generations. Like so many other Cotswold towns it was little affected by the Industrial Revolution in Britain and has to a great extent retained its mainly 17th century architectural harmony and its compact town centre. Many of its buildings are listed and many of its streets are curved; there are small squares and open areas, a striking skyline and ancient bridges to span the river with its attendant water meadows of grazing cattle.

The immediate surrounding land is fairly flat but the town itself stands amidst the gently rolling land near the southeastern edges of the Cotswold hills where Gloucestershire joins Wiltshire. From Tetbury it is about five miles to Malmesbury and Cirencester is around ten miles distant.

The historians have concluded that the mother of St. Guthlac was named Tetta. There was also another mention of Tetta, possibly the same person, who was Abbess of Winbourne and sister of King Ince or Ine of Wessex. Further, it is assumed that as

*Below: Down the famous steps at Tetbury*
*Right: The very handsome Town Hall*

early as AD680 there was a monastery in the vicinity headed by the Abbess Tetta and it is therefore felt that the name of Tetbury was, over a period of time, derived from the name Tetta. It is quite likely that this was the earliest Christian settlement in the county of Gloucestershire and while no trace of this Saxon monastery exists today, the town has claim to an ancient past.

King Ethelred had granted by charter certain land which was situated close to Tetta's minster to the Abbot of Malmesbury in AD681 and put a curse on those who should take away the land so granted. King Offa of Mercia then appeared on the scene, granting the land to his own monastery at Worcester after defeating the West Saxons at Bensington. From then on the tiny streams that flow along the southwestern side of the town became the line which divided Mercia and Wessex. For more than 1,000 years the boundary remained the same, the water dividing Gloucestershire and Wiltshire right up to the 1930s when the Fosse Way became the dividing line.

At the same time as the monastery stood, so also did a minster church and by the 8th century the presence of a Bishop was recorded. By 1086, the time of

Domesday, there was a priest at Tetbury which indicated that there must have been some kind of church present. At this time Tetbury was a prosperous farming community and together with the Manor of Upton it was owned by Roger de Ivre.

During the 12th century a Cistercian monastery had been founded and William de Braose or Bruce held the lordship. Around the turn of the century a charter encouraging the townsfolk to develop as merchants was granted by him, thus the agricultural village changed to town status. During the following generations William's descendants, who became the Earls of Berkeley, inherited the lordship and by the 17th century independence in stages was granted to the town, the manor and borough being sold to Tetbury's inhabitants in 1633.

Tetbury's fine parish church, dedicated to St. Mary, was rebuilt during the late 1700s having been damaged a hundred years earlier during bad weather. There seems to have been a long drawn out debate about whether it should be repaired or rebuilt but eventually a compromise was reached. The tower with its tall spire on top was left and the remainder was pulled down and a somewhat grander building than the previous church was built.

Unfortunately the spire was struck by lightning in 1789 and by 1891 it was found to be in a serious state of disrepair by which time the spire had leant over by almost 5ft. Both the tower and the spire were rebuilt in exactly the same design as the old using much of the original material, thus the tower and spire are of 15th century design but of more modern construction and are claimed to be amongst the tallest and most elegant in the land.

The church itself was one of the earliest of the Gothic revival churches. It is spacious, light and airy inside with large windows which give a certain elegance to its 120ft x 62ft x 42ft high interior. Its rather unusual design includes 'ambulatories' which are access passages to the pews in the aisle via the doors. This has been likened by some visitors to those in the old concert halls. In the nave are a pair of chandeliers of 1781 each designed to hold 36 candles, thus a good light was available in those days at Tetbury. A good light was very necessary as it was usually expected that over half the population, certainly of a country town like Tetbury, would attend church regularly. Whether they went because they wanted to or because they felt they ought to be seen to go is neither here nor there; the fact was that the congregation paid for their own seats. A

*The tall spire of St Mary's Church, Tetbury*

*Left: Long Street, Tetbury*

103

rich person, a woolstapler for example, paid the sum of £9 5s, presumably per annum, for his family's place in church. During later years, in 1848 to be exact, the little church for the poor opened its doors to accommodate the poor of the town who had for generations been crowded out of St. Mary's. The new church was St. Saviour's which was designed to accommodate 400 people. It was built in the street known as Cuckolds Knappside which was later called very simply New Church Street and at that time the cost of building the church was around £3,500. It was threatened with demolition in 1976 but after much protest it

*Church Street, Tetbury*

was saved and has since become a listed building within this conservation area.

Much of the town's development came about, as it did in many instances in the past, due to one or more forward thinking and benevolent individuals and in the case of Tetbury one of the main benefactors was William Romney. He was a native of the town who later became Knight, Alderman and Sheriff of the City of London. It is thought that he was a successful draper who held the position of alderman of various wards of the City during the early 1600s and who was knighted at Whitehall in 1603. He was also a director of the East India Company, becoming governor in 1601. It was he who instigated the search for the North West Passage and had much to do with the sending of Henry Hudson, after which the Hudson Bay Company was named, to discover the passage in 1610. Sir William Romney was undoubtedly a very wealthy person but he was also a generous one making donations to hospitals and to scholars. In his Will he left the lease of the tolls and monies from Tetbury's markets to the town's inhabitants, from which payments were made to the poor and for the employment of a schoolmaster.

Like most other towns of the Cotswolds, Tetbury had developed and prospered due to its location within this enormously rich wool producing area. By the close of the 14th century its markets became a centre for buying and selling of agricultural produce but wool was by far the biggest money maker and it was yet again the profits from wool sales and sales of wool products that formed the foundation for Tetbury's development. Prior to 1633 the town was owned by the Manor at Berkeley until it was bought by four wealthy wool merchants for £840. During the 16th century it was known as one of the best markets for yarn and for wool in the whole of Gloucestershire and many craftsmen worked at Tetbury

manufacturing cloth. Wool combing seemed to have taken place primarily to the west of the town centre in and around the aforementioned Cuckholds Knappside. During later developments in the manufacturing process the lack of a suitable water supply was to limit the town's growth, for the fulling mill required water for power just as the later development of steam powered processes for weaving was dependent on water. This was of course readily available in the steep sided valleys around Stroud where, by the 18th century, power driven machinery was to speed up the manufacturing processes very considerably. Tetbury therefore had to content itself with the simpler stages of production, sorting, combing and spinning for instance. It is for this reason that there is very little evidence in Tetbury of development during the Industrial Revolution and it is why so much of its older architecture is still intact. By the early 1800s this formerly important wool market had gone into steep decline, the last payment at the Market Hall for wool weighing being in 1815.

The Market Hall is just opposite The Snooty Fox. It is held aloft by eighteen stalwart pillars. Originally built in 1655, it was modified in 1817. Before its modification, when the whole of its upper storey was removed and one end enclosed to provide a fire station and a town prison, it must have looked even more handsome than it does today. Designed to be used for weighing wool the building was essentially functional.

Bacon and cheese merchants also developed in Tetbury and a special market served a wide area in both commodities. The large square known as The Chipping and surrounded by fine 18th century houses became its trade centre. Some historians have noted that it was possible that The Chipping was the site of an early monastery. There is no firm proof of this but over the centuries this has resulted in the old Manor House becoming known as the House that was built upon the Priory. The Manor House has been known as Hicket Court and more recently the house became the home of John Frampton, the Vicar of Tetbury.

From the northeastern corner of the square the well-known Chipping Steps descend to the Cirencester Road. At the head of the steps stands St. Michael's House, next to which are a couple of cottages, then the tiny Little Hall and on the same side is Oak House. Across The

Chipping stand The Manse, Stafford House and Berkeley House, all fine examples of 18th century architecture, while just beyond the narrow lane Eccles Court is now the Priory Nursing Home.

As the town expanded so it required road improvements and while certain roads had been improved during the 1500s and the users charged on a toll system, by the 1700s it was apparent that the turnpike Commissioners required an up to date bridge for crossing the river on the road to Bath. Thomas Webb built the resultant Bath Bridge in 1775 as the stone on the parapet explains. Previously the crossing was by

way of a ford after which extra horses were required to pull up the very steep Blackhorse Hill and into the town at West Street. The other bridge, formerly known as the Long Bridge, carried the road from Malmesbury across the River Avon. This crossing formed the border between Gloucester and Wiltshire and for this reason it became known as the Wiltshire Bridge.

Many years ago the old town was the home of numerous inns, some of which are still with us today. The White Hart, for instance, more recently known as The Snooty Fox, was recorded in 1594 and saw tremendous development during the

*The old road passes beneath the arches of the existing road*

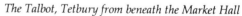

*The Talbot, Tetbury from beneath the Market Hall*

105

coaching days, being well placed on the routes to Bath and Oxford. From the middle of the last century many hunt balls were held in its assembly room and in 1921 the town's first cinema was held here.

At the eastern end of the Market Place is the former Talbot Hotel which was recorded in 1696 but possibly hosted Charles I in 1643. Like the White Hart it became a popular coaching inn but has recently been refurbished and is known as the Talbot Apartments, next to which is Crew House and then the Chantry House. Across the road on Gumstool Hill and dating from the late 17th century stands the Crown Inn. Formerly it was the Queen's Arms and later The Angel. Beyond it are a number of other fine old dwellings.

By chance Tetbury emerged during the late 18th century as being one of the fashionable hunting regions in southern England and today the surrounding farming land is a rich area through which the Beaufort Hunt frequently ride. Close by is Highgrove House, the home of Prince Charles, and closer to Minchinhampton is the home of the Princess Royal. Whilst in the town the visitor will no doubt notice a number of businesses with the triple feathered crest and the claim 'By Royal Appointment'.

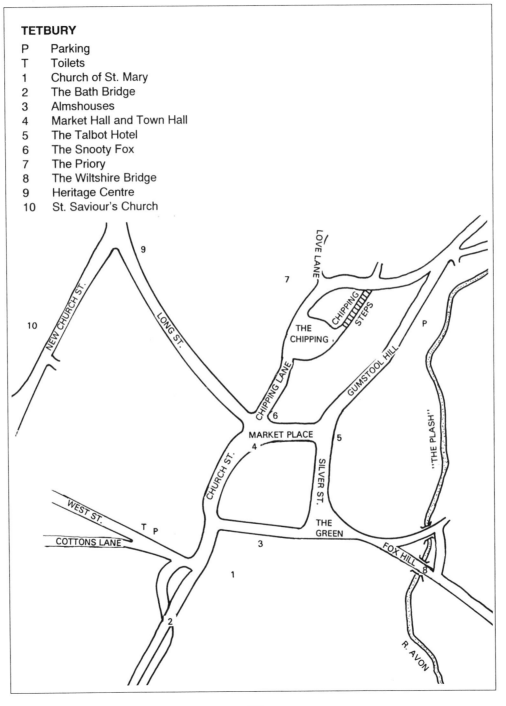

**TETBURY**

| | |
|---|---|
| P | Parking |
| T | Toilets |
| 1 | Church of St. Mary |
| 2 | The Bath Bridge |
| 3 | Almshouses |
| 4 | Market Hall and Town Hall |
| 5 | The Talbot Hotel |
| 6 | The Snooty Fox |
| 7 | The Priory |
| 8 | The Wiltshire Bridge |
| 9 | Heritage Centre |
| 10 | St. Saviour's Church |

# 17: Tewkesbury

At the confluence of the Rivers Avon and Severn, in the vale between the Cotswold hills and Malvern, stands Tewkesbury, a town with a history as romantic as any in England. During the more stormy days of this country's past it has, on a number of occasions, become the centre of where the future fate of England has been decided. Its streets have resounded to the clash of arms and the stench of war as Englishmen fell upon each other on more than one occasion. Murders have been committed and the powerful and influential done to death beside the ancient Town Cross. For almost 900 years its Abbey, built by Robert Fitzhamon, has stood watching over all through times of war and peace.

Tewkesbury has throughout the centuries catered for a variety of visitors including royalty, writers and artists. In addition to its history and architecture, the River Avon and the River Severn are always an attraction, especially during the summer months, for anglers, boaters and for those who just like to sit and stare.

Throughout recent centuries a small amount of Neolithic pottery has been found in and around Tewkesbury indicating that the area was inhabited about 2,500 BC, but until the arrival of the Romans little else is known about the residents of this area. When the Romans did arrive in this part of England, the natives of the region were the Dobunni tribe who were prepared to cooperate with the invaders. Thus within the areas around Tewkesbury, Cirencester and Gloucester at least life was reasonably harmonious. During this time there was a ford across the River Severn at Tewkesbury and it was probably this that was of most interest to the Romans as it provided a transport route to the land beyond. However Tewkesbury was for practical purposes far less important than either of the other two Roman cities and was not developed to the same extent as either of them.

During Saxon times Brictric was the last lord of Tewkesbury. He was a most important man in this part of southern England and was probably descended from the royal family of Wessex. His family owned vast areas of land throughout Gloucestershire, Devon and Somerset. However Tewkesbury was undoubtedly his largest Manor reaching from the River Severn to the Cotswold scarp. It covered close to 9,000 acres and while he had a hall at Oxenton his main residence was at Tewkesbury.

*The Abbey Mills*

There exists a possibility that Brictric was involved in a revolt against the Norman invaders nine years after the Battle of Hastings, as a result of which his lands were quickly divided up by the conquerors, the greatest part being allocated to Queen Maud, wife of the Conqueror. Before 1086, the time of Domesday, Maud made legal the establishment of a market at Tewkesbury thereby giving the townspeople the right to buy and sell produce and products on which the Lord of the Manor was paid a tax. As the market trade increased so did the town's importance.

To the north on Mythe Hill the Normans built a stronghold known as the Tute. It was a sentry position with good visibility between the River Avon and the River Severn and was constructed primarily to control raiders who ventured along these rivers. Shortly after the death of William I his son granted Tewkesbury to a strong supporter of his father, Robert Fitz-Hamon, and it was he who was responsible for the glorious architecture that the visitor sees in today's St. Mary's Abbey. He had decided that an abbey should be founded here. Both Worcester and Gloucester had fine abbey churches and the Abbey at Tewkesbury was the third in the series and was built in a similar architectural style. Robert Fitz-Hamon was one of the most powerful Norman nobles in the whole of England at this time but he was killed on a hunting trip in 1100. He was buried in the chapter house of his own, great new monastery. Later his body was moved to rest in the church and in 1241 a chantry chapel was constructed to his memory.

Both the Abbey church and the status of the Norman lords of Tewkesbury contributed to the town becoming so successful during the centuries that followed. One of the lords of Tewkesbury during this time was King John who in 1204

*The magnificent west end, Tewkesbury Abbey*

*The Abbot's Gateway, Tewkesbury Abbey*

spent Christmas in the town. His stay was apparently a very elaborate affair and the feasting was taken very seriously, so seriously in fact that around 4,500 pieces of crockery were specially bought for the occasion; no doubt a memorable Christmas was enjoyed by all his guests. A few years earlier, he had had improvements made to the Manor House but perhaps the best contribution he made to the town was the fine old bridge, which spanned the Avon, aptly named King John's Bridge.

The original timber bridge was constructed around 1205. During its lifetime it was known as the Mythe Bridge, an obvious name as it connects with the hill of the same name and at one time it was referred to as the Long Bridge. It was not until the 19th century that it inherited its grander title of King John's Bridge, the structure of which was extensively updated 38 years ago. The visitor will no doubt agree that the picturesque, multi-arched river crossing, surrounded by Tewkesbury's black and white architecture, is very worthy of its noble name.

At the corner of the High Street and close to the bridge is the Black Bear Inn which dates from the 12th century. It is claimed to be the oldest inn in the county. Just opposite are the handsome almshouses known as King John's Cottages.

When King John divorced Queen Isabel he relinquished the manor of Tewkesbury, and it passed into the hands of Gilbert de Clare whose family owned the manor for the next one hundred years. The de Clares were Earls of Hereford, Glamorgan and Gloucester and owned vast estates in these western and border counties, the family originally coming from East Anglia. During their time they were one of the most powerful families in southern England who would entertain up to 60 knights at the manor house of Tewkesbury, not to mention having the King of England to stay

on a number of occasions. Henry III stayed here in 1236 whilst concluding a treaty with the Welsh. Forty years later Edward I, who finally subdued the Welsh and built his string of castles to govern them, stayed at Tewkesbury whilst negotiating with Alexander III of Scotland. Sadly the place where all this history was made is itself no more. It is generally supposed that the old building stood not too far away from the manor vineyard which today forms the recreation ground of Vineyard Park.

After Bannockburn Gilbert de Clare lay dead. His death was followed the next year by that of his wife. The Crown then owned the estate until 1325 when the Despensers inherited Tewkesbury and continued to rule over it for a further one hundred years. Much of their legacy to the town is the rebuilding of the Abbey and its roof. Much of the vaulting and many windows that exist today are regarded as having been financed by this powerful family.

It may come as a surprise to find that Tewkesbury of all places should be involved in the War of the Roses, which after all was a duel between the houses of Yorkshire and Lancashire, so far north as to have no influence on this southwestern part of England.

Richard Neville, Earl of Warwick was married to the Countess Ann who held Tewkesbury. Her husband became known as the 'king maker' due to his inability to make a decision and stick to it with regard to whom he favoured to rule England, the House of York or the House of Lancaster. The Earl of Warwick was killed fighting alongside the Lancastrians at the Battle of Barnet early in 1471 leaving Tewkesbury to the Duke of Clarence who was a Yorkist sympathizer; thus Tewkesbury was drawn into the struggle. The Yorkist Edward IV was on the throne, while Queen Margaret of Anjou, wife of Henry VI of Lancaster, who was imprisoned in the Tower, had been

refused entry into the city of Gloucester and had arrived with her army at Tewkesbury. She arranged her forces on the ridge of Gupshill just to the south of the town and departed to the Abbey. Her son Prince Edward of Lancaster, the Duke of Somerset and the Earl of Devonshire were her commanders. King Edward was three miles away close by Tredington where his army was commanded by himself, the Duke of Clarence, the Duke of Gloucester and Lord Hastings. The King based his battle plan on the same formula he had used so successfully at the Battle of Barnet three weeks earlier. He rallied his forces, made an

*Abbey Lawn Cottages where Gander Lane joins Church Street*

*The House of the Golden Key*

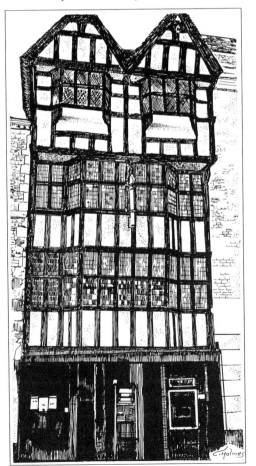

early start and arriving on high ground they advanced toward the waiting Lancastrians near to the Manor of Gupshill. The Lancastrian position was strong but the King strengthened the position of his army by dispatching 200 horsemen to a tree covered hill to his left, known today as Tewkesbury Park. He then provoked his adversaries into making a rash move, confusion followed and eventually the horsemen saw their opportunity. At this unexpected attack from the flank the opposition fled and were routed in Bloody Meadow while heading for Lower Lode ferry. Some Lancastrians who made for the town itself were drowned in the Abbey millpond and others were chased into the Abbey where the fighting continued. The outcome was a disaster for the Lancastrians. Most of the dead were buried close by with the nobles being buried in the Abbey. The leaders who survived were put to death in the market place. But the carnage was not just contained to Tewkesbury. A number of the Lancastrians who escaped after the battle were pursued as far as the village of Didbrook, not far from Winchcombe. They had sought refuge in the church but were slaughtered within the building despite the calls from the clergy to spare them. When the Abbot of Hailes Abbey heard of this desecration of the church he had it demolished and a new one was built at his own expense.

Ironically only 14 years after this battle, Richard III, the last of the Yorkist Royalty, was defeated at Bosworth and Henry Tudor established the Lancastrians as the rulers of England once again.

Today the town is famous for its black and white architecture and for me, as a pen and ink illustrator, the timber framed buildings that signified the growing prosperity of the 15th, 16th and 17th centuries are a particular delight. In the

*The Royal Hop Pole*

110

main the dwellings at Tewkesbury were of two storeys but there were exceptions, a third storey being added later in some cases. At Tewkesbury there seem to be few rear access roads to the developments of this period and because of this many buildings have an entrance at the side thereby giving carts and animals access to the yards and outbuildings. The visitor will find such buildings off Church Street and in other parts of the town.

It is worth mentioning just a few of those buildings which are outstanding or unique. The Ancient Grudge in the High Street is quite flamboyant with its herring-bone studding, its timbers being placed close together in a herring-bone pattern. This is probably a false front added to a building which could date as far back as 1500. On the upper floors the bay windows, inserted during the 19th century, are quite modern by comparison. There are a number of properties in the town having upper storeys which overhang the ground floor. Occasionally a building with an overhang on more than one elevation can be seen. The House of the Golden Key and the Clarence House opposite are just further examples of the town's fine architecture.

Along Church Street the scene is similar and around the Royal Hop Pole Hotel and across to the Berkeley Arms little changes. The Royal Hop Pole was known a couple of centuries ago as the New Inn. It was here that Dickens' Pickwick stopped to take refreshment. The plaque on the wall refers the visitor to *Pickwick Papers* Chapter 50 and it reads: "At the Hop Pole, Tewkesbury, they stopped to dine, upon which occasion there was more Bottled Ale, with some more Madeira and some Port besides and here the Case Bottle was replenished for the fourth time. Under the influence of these combined stimulants, Mr. Pickwick and Mr. Ben Allen fell fast asleep for thirty miles while Bob and Mr. Weller sang duets in the dickey."

The Abbey Cottages in Church Street rate amongst the finest of the town's examples of 15th century architecture. Restored around 1970 by the Abbey Lawn Trust they were originally built by the Abbey as shops and 17 of the original development of 23 survive today. One of them is the Little Museum which has been restored to its former self, with window shutters that double as a street counter and a living room with an open fire. The house had one upstairs room, a further room being added behind the living room at a later date. The windows of course were devoid of glass but wooden shutters kept in the warmth at night.

Unlike the vast majority of 'true' Cotswold towns Tewkesbury, lying to the west of the enormously wealthy wool producing region of medieval England, had to rely, apart from her market, on other forms of income. This it seems was a mixture of different products. Textile production formed the basis of it but shoe-making and leather working was one of the Tewkesbury trades. There were tanners, skinners, glovers and saddle makers together with all the ancillary crafts and tradespeople. Most of the surplus agricultural produce from the surrounding region was 'exported' by river or road to places such as Bristol, Bath and the like. At one time the growing and producing of mustard and mustard products was very prominent.

The land surrounding Tewkesbury is flat, so much so that at times the town appears to have been developed as an island adhering to a small area of reliable firm ground. Access to the town has through necessity been across a simplified form of dyke system not unlike the vast areas of similar countryside in East Anglia.

Back in the 16th century the town was dependent on seven bridges, some of which were only footbridges, to convey the traffic in and out of the town and across this marshy, low lying area. But the River Severn was also an important means of transporting wheat, malt, corn and coal from the forest of Dean. In the 16th century boat building became part of the town's industries and slipways and the town quay were developed on the old Avon. The boat building tradition continued during the dark days of the Second World War when motor torpedo boats were built in small numbers in secluded local yards. Nowadays this industry has declined and the Healing's mill at present occupies much of the old quayside.

By 1642 the English Civil War had made Tewkesbury a centre of attack and counter attack. The town was at various times occupied by the opposing forces of the Cavaliers and Parliamentarians. Street fighting became commonplace between the opposing sides and during the early days of 1643 the town changed hands four times within two months. The town was valuable as it commanded the bridge over the Avon and a couple of ferries which provided links across the Severn. The town itself was naturally fortified to a great extent by its surrounding river defences.

Sir William Russell occupied the town in April 1643 when a two pronged attack was mounted by the Parliamentarians. One group advanced up the River Severn and crossed the marshy area known as The Ham but found the River Mill Avon blocking the way. By Lower Lode another force reached the drawbridge crossing the River Swilgate. After some fleeing on the Royalist part the majority of their troops regrouped and faced the Parliamentarians at Ripple, just to the north. The running battle finished at Mythe, many soldiers being drowned in the River Severn and while the slaughter proved to be inconclusive militarily, the town yet again was in the hands of the

*The old Hat Shop in Church Street*

Cromwellians. It was as if history was repeating itself again and reminding the town of the War of the Roses all those years before.

During the 17th century and after the ravages of the Civil War the town slowly recovered as did most of England. In Tewkesbury there was only a small amount of street frontage available for housing development and consequently older wide plots within the town were split up and many large dwellings were subdivided in an attempt to better use the firm ground. As with many towns throughout the land much false fronting of older properties was

*Bystanders waiting for a parade to pass the Town Museum in Barton Street, Tewkesbury*

carried out in order to present an external appearance of the later styles of architecture. While the older trades and everyday businesses continued to flourish it was without doubt the influence of Elizabeth I with her preference for stockings of the newer knitted designs, as opposed to the older hose of cloth, which set the town on the upward spiral of development which continued for generations.

The stocking knitting frame was invented by William Lee and in 1619 John Sewell, who resided at Bisley in the southern Cotswolds, came to Tewkesbury as a freeman hosier. Twenty-three years later another hosier of renown, William Croft, was established in the town. The river also contributed to the growth in the town's fortunes with the increase in waterborne freight. Soon boats were able to pass beyond King John's Bridge as William Sandys made the river navigable right up to Evesham. By 1672 ships up to 30 tons could berth alongside the quay at Stratford on Avon, close to where the Memorial Theatre stands today. A navigable river and good quay facilities were of course vital to future generations as the hosiery business developed to form the backbone of the town's economy. The industry developed steadily from the early 1700s and eventually all manner of cotton garments were being produced locally. Shortly freemen silk weavers left London to settle and develop in Tewkesbury. It seemed that whatever else was spun either at home or abroad, the production of Tewkesbury could match it price for price and by the end of the 18th century approximately one fortieth of all knitting frames in England were churning out their products at Tewkesbury. By 1825, however, the industry was in decline and 15 years later fashions had changed. The boom years were over and newer cotton production techniques had brought to an end this period of the town's development.

But what of Tewkesbury today?

The Tudor House Hotel in the High Street was for a time a Dissenters Academy. This was a place of higher education for men who were not allowed into England's most famous universities, i.e. Cambridge or Oxford, as they were not members of the Church of England. Following this in the 19th century it was a girls' boarding school.

Not many visitors to Tewkesbury will be aware that at one time it was felt that the town should be launched into the fashionable and profitable 'spa town' business. After all spring water flowed from the earth just a mile or so to the south of the Ashchurch Road. The land concerned was owned by Richard Smithsend who built a house, Walton Spa, but whilst the pump was apparently frequently used it was insufficient to grow into a real business as had been the case at other towns. George III had been a visitor to the town in the summer of 1788 after taking the waters at Cheltenham and no doubt this and a number of other visits to Tewkesbury by His Majesty promoted thoughts of what he did for Cheltenham, he could also do for Tewkesbury. This, however, was not to be and in more recent years the old house was demolished in order to make way for modern developments.

The reader will by now be well aware that to a great extent Tewkesbury would have long ago become an island if it were not for the ability of the bridge builder. The huge flat area of The Ham had always been and to some extent is still a problem with regard to suitable access and flooding close to the town. One of the finest engineers known to England was at that time constructing the magnificent bridge which crossed the Menai Straits linking the island of Anglesey to the coast of North Wales. Telford was persuaded to come to Tewkesbury to assess the situation. The result of his visit was the construction of the

Mythe Bridge which was opened in 1826 and consisted of six main cast-iron ribs which supported the road carrying pillars. It was a standard design which Telford was to apply to different situations at different times. It has been suggested by modern biographers that this bridge is one of the finest examples of cast-iron construction techniques left standing.

Of all the town's architecture the Abbey must be the most outstanding. Its huge 132ft high by 46ft square tower is claimed to be the largest in existence. It was built at different times being finally completed in 1163. The battlements and pinnacles were added much later in about 1600.

To the right of the entrance porch are the 15th century remains of the Abbot's Lodgings which extended to the battlemented gateway, the former private entrance to the lodgings.

The west front is also imposing. With its deep recessed arch 62ft high and 34ft wide it is the highest in the country. The window was added in 1686. No doubt this fine building would be even finer but most of the building to the south right up to the tiny River Swilgate was demolished at the Dissolution in 1541 and only a small part of the former cloisters remains. At the same time the Lady Chapel at the eastern end of the Abbey was also pulled down.

As befits such a noble piece of Norman architecture the nave seems filled with 14 huge circular columns measuring almost 20ft in diameter. They are said to be the tallest in England. Above the arches is an early designed triforium while the stone vaulting of the aisles dates from the latter part of the 13th century. On the south wall above the War Memorial and above the north door are the remaining corbels which would have supported the original timber roof in Norman times. Originally the monastery was divided from the parish church of Tewkesbury by a stone screen set close to the second column from the east in the nave.

On the right in the ambulatory are two tombs within the wall, one of which is of Abbot Alan who was previously at Canterbury but came to Tewkesbury after the murder of Thomas a' Becket. In the Choir is the Milton organ, the case of which was constructed around 1580 at Magdalene College, Oxford. In 1654 Oliver Cromwell had it removed and installed at Hampton Court. In 1660 with the restoration of the monarchy the organ returned to Oxford being purchased by Tewkesbury in 1727.

At the centre of the tower is a brass plate which reads, "Here lies Edward Prince of Wales, cruelly slain while still a youth, on May 4th 1471. Alas, the fury of men. Thou art the sole light of thy mother, and the last hope of the flock." It refers to the only son of Henry VI and Margaret of Anjou, who died or was murdered soon after the battle of Tewkesbury.

At more than 13ft by 3ft 6ins the High Altar at Tewkesbury is the longest of all England's medieval altars. Its top of Purbeck marble dating from 1239 was buried to save it from desecration during the Dissolution of the Monasteries. Recovered during the early 1600s it was used as a communion table only to be cut in half in 1730 and used as seating in the porch. It was returned to its rightful place as recently as 1879.

Finally toward the east end of the ambulatory and close to the remnant of a screen dating from the 14th century is an iron grating in the floor. Below this is buried the remains of the Duke of Clarence and his wife. He was the Lord of the Manor of Tewkesbury and the brother of Edward IV and Richard III and he was reputed to have died by drowning, not at sea but in a butt of Malmsey wine.

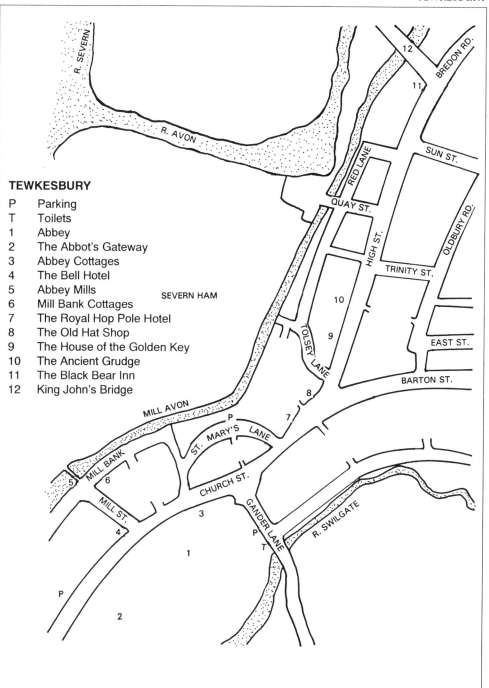

**TEWKESBURY**

P  Parking
T  Toilets
1  Abbey
2  The Abbot's Gateway
3  Abbey Cottages
4  The Bell Hotel
5  Abbey Mills
6  Mill Bank Cottages
7  The Royal Hop Pole Hotel
8  The Old Hat Shop
9  The House of the Golden Key
10 The Ancient Grudge
11 The Black Bear Inn
12 King John's Bridge

# 18: Winchcombe

The centre of Winchcombe is quite compact. For the most part its varied buildings line the roadway as it rises, curves and gently falls presenting a rich mixture of stone and part timber framed dwellings, many of which still retain well worn stone steps with metal hand rails, stone tiled roofs and dormer windows. It is not as well known as some Cotswold towns nor is it so touristy as Broadway, Burford or Bourton-on-the-Water. Its prettiest part is probably in cottage-lined Vineyard Street as it sweeps down to the River Isbourne and up to the gatehouse of the handsome Sudeley Castle within its lovely grounds.

It seems quite incredible that other than three modernised buildings with their roots in the 15th century and known as a whole as 'The Abbey', little remains of what must have been a very substantial and prosperous Abbey at Winchcombe in days gone by. The old abbey would have stood close to the present day Church of St Peter, on the site occupied by The Green which faces Abbey Terrace. Excavations to the east of St Peter's Lane confirm the existence of a large central tower but other than some of the stonework of Norman origin, which is kept in the church, and a doorway into the church there is not much left of this once important building and centre of learning.

During Saxon times Winchcombe was the capital of Mercia. The King of Mercia was Kenulf who, in AD789, founded an abbey on the site of a former nunnery which had been constructed by Offa only a short time earlier. On the death of Kenulf, his son Kenelm, who was still a child of seven years of age, became King of Mercia, and no doubt much elaborated over the centuries, his martyrdom led to the early establishment of a town at Winchcombe.

The story goes that Kenelm had an elder half sister, Quendrida, who felt that with her younger brother out of the way the Kingdom would be hers and with this in mind she persuaded one Askobert, a tutor abbot, to do away with the boy king. Whilst out hunting the child was tricked into a diversion through secluded woodland where he was murdered. With the usual high drama of early religious tales, the story tells of a white dove flying from the boy's beheaded body only to reappear a year or so later with a message for the Pope who was celebrating mass in Rome. After translation the message delivered to the Pope read: "In Clent cow-pasture, under a thorn, Of Head bereft lies Kenelm, King born." This information was passed to the

*Studeley Castle beyond the trees in springtime*

114

English Kings and in due course the boy's body was located with the aid of a white cow near a thorn bush, whereupon a spring of water duly rose from the spot. The body was carried from the woodland of Clent in Worcestershire (some tales tell of the body being recovered from Shropshire) where it had been located to Winchcombe, the monks setting down their load close to Sudeley a couple of miles from the town. Here a second spring gushed forth. Later this water, which it was said to have healing properties, had a well house built over it and a chapel was added. This was later demolished during the 19th century.

This elaborate tale continues with the wicked sister Quendrida losing her eyesight as a result of the vengeance of the Almighty when the procession bearing the body reached Winchcombe. During the years following these events the Abbey developed rapidly. Unfortunately the Danes destroyed it in AD985 but it was rebuilt and rededicated to St Kenelm by Oswald, the Bishop of Worcester and it continued to attract pilgrims to the town in great numbers, especially as it was for many on their route to nearby Hailes Abbey. Under his management the abbey flourished and at that time became a great centre of learning likened to the other leading centres of the day. The demise of the abbey came at the hand of Lord Seymour in 1539, when it appears that nothing less than complete demolition of the abbey was good enough for him. He obviously carried out his brief with vim and vigour!

The Church of St Peter at Winchcombe is a good example of late Perpendicular church architecture. It is a large church with a 90ft high battlement topped tower with eight crocketed pinnacles which still bear the scars of shot and shrapnel from the Civil War. Atop the tower is an enormous weathercock which came originally from the Church of St Mary, Radcliffe at Bristol.

The porch is gracefully vaulted and a room above it, complete with stone fireplace, was built to accommodate the resident priest. The church, which is spacious and quite airy, dates from the latter half of the 15th century when Abbot William of Winchcombe commenced construction. It was later continued by Rolf le Botelar. At that time it seems that size rather than attention to intricate detail was important. This has resulted in an interior of dignified if somewhat plain appearance. The nave with its large bays is as wide as the chancel, in which there is a large east window.

Within the building there is much evidence of the connection between the church, the local families of prominence and those who have in their day made contributions to the church such as the Merrymans, Blebys, Chadbornes and Harveys. Also within the church and quite fittingly so, are two ancient coffins of stone which were recovered during excavations in 1815. They are almost certainly those of the Abbey's founder King Kenulf and his son King Kenelm who, following his death at the hands of his half sister, became a saint. When this coffin was found it contained the remains of a knife which was thought to be the original murder weapon.

In the church's south aisle is the Churchwarden's chest. This was used for the safekeeping of the accounts, the church plate and the parish registers. The original 12th century chest inside it was made by hollowing out a huge log of oak. In the north aisle the oak door with the carved initials R.K. standing for Richard Kydderminster is one of the few remains of the former Abbey. The alms box is 16th century and had three locks to it, as was the standard practice insisted upon by Edward VI in 1547. The box could be opened by the vicar and two church wardens each of whom had a key. The very attractive font at

St Peter's dates from 1643 and the colourful cover is the original.

Just across the road from the church and at the head of Queen Square is the Jacobean House of 1618 which was formerly the Kings School, founded by Edward VI for ten local boys. Beyond which in the adjacent narrow Almshouse Lane leading down toward Mill Lane are the Chandos Almshouses. These dwellings were built by Lady Chandos in 1573, originally to house twelve of the town's poor women, and were rebuilt in 1841. The original coats of arms are still decipherable and the buildings are decorated with their own gargoyle.

*The Jacobean house in Queen's Square and St Peter's church*

Lovely old cottages line both sides of Vineyard Street as it dips steeply down toward the River Isbourne, crosses the bridge and climbs steadily up toward Sudeley Castle. Originally it led to the vineyards owned by the Abbey but it was at one time known as Duck Street, for it was here that the ducking stool was situated down by the river.

Beyond Vineyard Street and to the right of Abbey Terrace is Dent's Terrace, a row of clean cut Victorian dwellings designed by Gilbert Scott. The whole row of dwellings was built on the cemetery of the former abbey. Beyond is Abbey Terrace where

*Dent's Terrace*

during the 18th and 19th century a number of houses were constructed on older foundations. Facing the Jacobean House the Lloyds Bank building was erected on the site of the original Mercian Palace.

Formerly used as a market hall the ground floor of the Town Hall, which was built in 1853, is now home of the Tourist Information Centre. The Folk and Police Museum is housed on the first floor. Outside are the old town stocks but unlike most others the Winchcombe stocks can accommodate three and half offenders, there being seven leg holes. At one time a whipping post stood close by.

Almost opposite the Town Hall is a building known as the Wesley House as John Wesley the evangelist is said to have stayed here on one of his visits to Winchcombe. Even better known in the town is the building that was formerly the old George Hotel. It is easily recognisable as a black and white timber framed building which has in recent years been converted into apartments. It was built in 1490 by Richard Kydderminster, who was the Abbot of the Abbey during Henry VII's reign, to provide accommodation for the huge numbers of pilgrims who were travelling to Winchcombe's Abbey of St Kenelm and beyond to the Abbey at Hailes. At this period in England's history Winchcombe was becoming a very close rival to Canterbury in its religious importance. The building still retains part of the Gallery which used to run around the central courtyard and the initials of Richard Kydderminster are still to be seen carved on the doorway. Beside the former George Hotel is the Abbots House with the coat of arms of the Abbot below one of the upper windows.

The High Street soon dips down and curves as it becomes Hailes Street, formerly known as the Pilgrims Way. Here there stands a most interesting mixture of

architecture from different periods in history. Stone, timber frame and brick make a pleasing combination of structures where shops fit in well with restaurants and tea shops and where the private dwellings have names such as Mercia (the former Wheatsheaf pub) with an overhanging first floor and Hwicci, an ancient name of a sub-kingdom of the pagan Saxon King Penda.

Opposite the Sun Inn in North Street an 18th century Phoenix Fire Insurers plaque is secured to the upper wall of the bookshop of the same name. This indicated to the local fire brigade that in the event of a fire if this building was saved it was insured and that they would be duly rewarded. Beyond, with stone mullioned windows and arched doorway, is the 15th century White Lion.

Close to the left corner of North Street, The Gate, which is a private dwelling, has an interesting history. It was formerly known as the Gate Inn and was said to possess a natural spring of water which, during the mid 1800s, was claimed to be as good a spa as Cheltenham's. It was developed as a hydropathic hotel for this period when 'taking the waters' became very fashionable. However here it did not seem to have caught on, for before long the building was operating as a coffee house. Until recent years the old sign was still visible and read: "This gate hangs well and hinders none, refresh and pay and travel on." For me one of Winchcombe's most interesting old buildings is the former old farmhouse at the corner of Malthouse Lane. Dating from the 16th century and now known as the Old Corner Cupboard Inn, it has a connection with Winchcombe's industry of paper making but was given its name during its time as an inn because of its many corner cupboards.

Back in the mid 1700s John Durham, the owner of the old farmhouse, became prosperous in the Winchcombe paper production business for this was the town's

main industry at that time. He died in 1759 leaving the house to his daughter Mary who married the town's apothecary William Reynolds.

Paper making had been developed at three different mills: blue bagging or sugar paper was manufactured at Lower Mill, writing paper was produced at Upper Mill while Middle Mill was where packing and brown paper were produced. It was a very labour intensive process entailing much hands-on work. A pulp was produced from strips of pre-cut rag or linen by beating with an iron mallet against a metal plate and mixing in water. By 1826 paper making machinery had been installed at Upper Mill and a few years later Middle Mill was entirely updated. Lower Mill however became a corn mill in 1836, but long before the turn of the century it became a private dwelling. By 1876 the company of Evans, Aland & Co. owned the whole of the local paper making business.

The town also had a small silk mill, hence the name today of Silk Lane. The mill used was a former corn mill and was converted by Mr. Barbury in 1820 or thereabouts. Within a thirty year period this three storey building was providing employment for about 100 women and children. In the main their task was to 'throw' the silk, the children being employed to change bobbins. Its success, using almost slave labour, was short lived and the silk industry in Winchcombe closed in 1872.

During earlier times an even more successful industry had been the illegal production of tobacco at Winchcombe. Sir Walter Raleigh's association with the not

too distant Brockhampton is often suggested as the reason why tobacco production became popular in the first place in this part of England. John Stratford is normally attributed as being the founder member of the industry, for an industry it became early in the 1600s. At this time he was leasing out around 100 acres of land and is reputed to have employed about 200 people on its cultivation. It was said that a barn at Postlip Hall was used at the time for wetting and drying the leaves and that tobacco warehouses were developed in the town's North Street. Winchcombe at the time had become a very depressed area

and to the labour force thus employed, tobacco became a 'God send', bringing to the masses a means of survival. Unfortunately the government was primarily concerned with creating a very lucrative monopoly for the tobacco being produced in the southern part of the New World, Virginia. A proclamation was duly issued making English production of tobacco illegal but while John Stratford seemed to obey the law, turning instead to the production of flax, others defied the ban and the crops continued to employ a large labour force. What is more, packhorses were crossing the wolds and illegally

*Above left: The stocks at Winchcombe*
*Left: 15th century seal from Hailes Abbey*

*Right: Timber frame and stone cottages in Hailes Street*

transporting the leaves to London. Thus whilst it was against the law it was a strong industry which was well supported in and around the town. Together with the production of flax it is thought that close to a third of the local population was employed in the industry at that time. By 1654 Winchcombe had a 300 strong force of men to protect the crop from damage from government officers and four years later a party of government troops were assaulted and beaten off as they tried to destroy the valuable crop. By the late 1600s however the government had successfully destroyed the industry and gradually due to the

increasing supply from the colonies with the consequent fall in price, it was no longer profitable to cultivate tobacco in the Winchcombe area. A reminder of those distant days is the name of Tobacco Close which is a street in the town.

Most visitors to Winchcombe find the not too distant Hailes Abbey well worth a visit, for after all Winchcombe's Abbey is no longer standing but at least at Hailes there is a graceful reminder of the past.

The Cistercian order was first established at Waverley in Surrey and they were one of those orders who developed, from the 11th century onwards, an austere form of religious life. The Abbey at Hailes was formed as a result, so it seems, of a rather dangerous sea crossing during bad weather by Richard, Earl of Cornwall who was returning from fighting in the Holy Land. The weather was so bad and the sea so forceful that during October of 1242 he probably muttered words to the effect, "God, if I get out of this alive I will build you an abbey." The Almighty spared him and so Richard kept his promise and in due course an Abbey was built. In 1246 twenty monks and ten lay preachers had arrived at Hailes from Beaulieu in Hampshire and they were duly set to work to construct this vast new building. On 5th November 1251 in front of the King, Queen Eleanor, the Earl Richard and a large company of nobles and bishops, with much ceremony the Abbey was dedicated.

In 1270 Edmund, the second son of Earl Richard, presented the community with a phial of red-coloured liquid which was claimed to have been brought from the Count of Flanders in 1267 as a genuine sample of holy blood. A Shrine was quickly built to house the special sample and in due

*The elegant ruins of Hailes Abbey, near Winchcombe*

*Above right: Cottages in Vinery Road,*
*Winchcombe*
*Right: One of the Winchcombe gargoyles*

course the Abbey became a special place for the pilgrims to visit. In fact it became one of the most important pilgrimage centres throughout England at that time. In 1538 after many years of commercial success it was discovered that the Holy Blood of Hailes was but a con trick and on 24th November of that year the Bishop of Rochester, who was preaching at St Paul's Cross, declared that the phial was a mixture of honey clarified with saffron and this was proved before the King and Council. This proved to be the end of Hailes Abbey. In 1542 the Crown, who by then owned the property, sold it to one Richard Andrews

shortly after which the buildings were demolished. Thus our generation is fortunate indeed to be able to enjoy the graceful remains of this great Abbey of yesteryear.

Originally commenced by John de Sudeley as early as the 12th century, Sudeley Castle was inherited by Ralph Boteler during the 15th century and under his supervision much expansion and development took place. During the War of the Roses the castle surrendered and passed into the hands of Edward IV. Since then it has had a succession of famous visitors including Henry VIII, Anne Boleyn and Catherine of Aragon. Catherine Parr lived here as a child as did Elizabeth I and Queen Mary.

After a varied selection of owners the castle eventually passed into the possession of the brother of Catherine Parr (the last wife of Henry VIII who is buried in the chapel at Sudeley). In 1554 the owner was Sir John Brydes, soon to become Lord Chandos of Sudeley, within whose family the castle remained until 1644 when it became the property of the Parliamentarians. Charles I had made it his headquarters but after his execution the Cromwellians damaged it so badly that it became a ruin. Much of its stonework, as

with Winchcombe's Abbey in earlier centuries, was confiscated by local people and found its way into the structure of many of the town's buildings.

In 1830 it was bought by the Dent family who restored the castle buildings, filled it with paintings and a host of other treasures and developed the splendid gardens.

Beyond Sudeley Castle, high up on a nearby hillside, is Belas Knapp. This is one of the better preserved of the Stone Age burial mounds of the Cotswolds and here much of its drystone walling is original. This 180ft long mound is around 4,000 years old and has entrances of 'crawl through' dimensions together with a large but false entrance to the north. It is thought that this could have been intended to confuse evil spirits as to the position of those buried inside, or it may have been built for the purpose of confusing grave robbers. Opened in the 1860s, 38 skeletons were found here together with some Roman remains.

To most people the initials G.W.R. are synonymous with the old Great Western Railway company before the days of nationalisation. Perhaps the Gloucester and Warwickshire Railway Company's name

*Spring sunshine at Studeley Castle*

*North Street, Winchcombe*

was carefully chosen to fit the old G.W.R. initials, I don't know, but this certainly is a thriving steam railway. It is an added attraction for visitors to Winchcombe and to Broadway, especially those with children for it is easily accessible from both places. It runs on the former Great Western Railway track bed from Toddington past Hailes Abbey to Gretton and passes through the cutting to the mouth of the Greet Tunnel which, at 693yds long, is one of the longest on any preserved railway in Britain. Except for the odd special day openings the G.W.R. only runs during the summer months, but with plans in hand to extend to Broadway and build a new station, who knows what the future holds for the railway and its dedicated enthusiasts. At some time it may be possible to travel to Stratford on Avon and beyond. I wish the G.W.R. well.

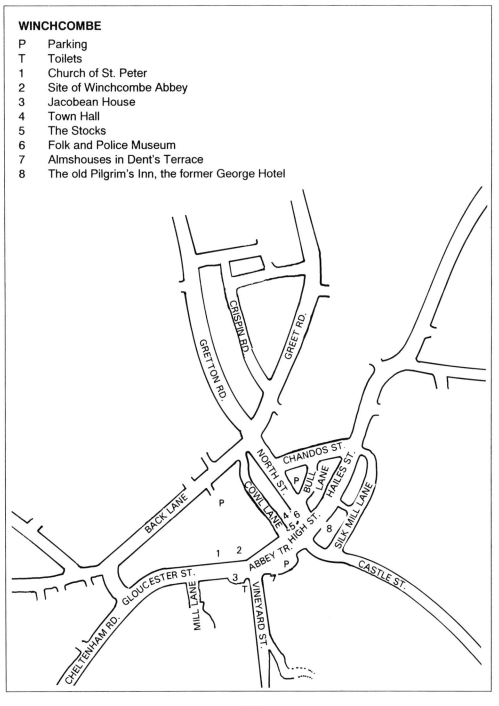

**WINCHCOMBE**

P     Parking
T     Toilets
1     Church of St. Peter
2     Site of Winchcombe Abbey
3     Jacobean House
4     Town Hall
5     The Stocks
6     Folk and Police Museum
7     Almshouses in Dent's Terrace
8     The old Pilgrim's Inn, the former George Hotel

# 19: Woodstock

*The old stocks, Woodstock*

A stockaded settlement within woodland is the simplest way of describing how the town of Woodstock came by its name. Today it is quite difficult to imagine that before the Norman Conquest most of what we know as the county of Oxfordshire was in fact a combination of huge forests. From Wychwood through Cornbury and Woodstock it was almost continuously forested apart from along the fertile valleys and the areas of marsh and swamp land. It was during this period that Woodstock gained popularity with Anglo Saxon royalty.

Previously there had been local Romano British settlements. Akeman Street, the Roman road, had crossed part of today's Blenheim Park and in the neighbouring areas the remains of Roman villas have been excavated. Toward the end of the 9th century it is believed that King Alfred may have had a royal residence here. King Ethelred, a century or so later, is said to have held council at Woodstock where he issued a decree for the maintenance of peace throughout the land.

By the time of Domesday Woodstock was referred to as a forest of the King, being reserved for hunting, and under the Normans the rights of those who lived in the clearings of the forest were quickly eroded with swift, sharp punishment for any who disobeyed the new rules. The youngest son of William the Conqueror was Henry I, who early in the 12th century built a manor at Woodstock and enclosed an area of parkland with a stone wall of 7 miles in circumference. He proceeded to stock this enclosure with all manner of wild animals in readiness for the sport of large scale, organised hunting. He is also attributed with founding Old Woodstock which sits on the hill close to the River Glyme. It is said of Henry I that he was not attracted to Woodstock entirely because of its excellent

hunting facilities but partly due to the gathering of wise and learned men who had joined together at not too distant Oxford; this was of course many years before the founding of any University. Henry I it seems was generally thought to be of a wise and scholarly nature, a very able ruler who brought some kind of order and meaning to turbulent England at that time. Unfortunately his stabilising influence on the country was short lived as on his death and with his only son drowned, his daughter Matilda and his nephew Stephen became rival claimants to the throne. War broke out and Woodstock held for Matilda until she escaped from the castle at Oxford but under Stephen the feudal barons lived like local war lords pillaging the land as they pleased while building themselves fine castles and residences. Sanity did not reassert itself in England until the reign of Matilda's son Henry II, who raised the prestige of the country to new heights within Europe by the razing of the baronial castles and setting in motion a reform of law and order. Under his jurisdiction the Assize of Woodstock dealt with the code of the forest and to these councils came many important and prominent people. It is worth mentioning at this point that Henry II also had a weakness in the form of a 'lady'. The legend of 'Fair Rosamund' is Woodstock's own version of Romeo and Juliet, a romance that was destined to have a tragic ending. In brief, King Henry II visited Woodstock not entirely to hunt but also to visit his mistress who was the daughter of Walter de Clifford. They met secretly at a bower or hunting lodge known as Everswell, which was designed around a spring with three pools. As his visits became increasingly frequent Henry II's Queen, Eleanor of Aquitaine became increasingly suspicious. She therefore visited Woodstock herself in 1176 and decided to solve the problem once and for all time by offering her husband's lover

a choice; after all they were both ladies! The choice was either a dagger or poison. Rosamund chose the latter, thus the problem was no more and the King's visits to the town were much reduced. This then is the tale that romantics would have us believe but it is quite readily accepted that Henry II visited his mistress quite openly whilst his queen was held as a virtual prisoner. Fair Rosamund died later of natural causes and was buried at Godstow Nunnery where her body was said to lie beneath the high altar. History has worked its magic and the tale of Fair Rosamund, whether true or false, is well recorded.

In order to accommodate the new visitors to the town new and commodious hostelries had to be constructed at Woodstock and thus began the development of the earlier settlement. The Manor by this time had been enlarged and had its own chapel while Woodstock itself developed outside the park gates and provided suitable dwellings and lodgings for the Royal retinue. A weekly market and a three day fair on the feast of St. Matthew was established.

A short time after the signing of the Magna Carta King John was said to have stayed here, for it seems he was a fairly regular visitor. His son, the pious Henry III, was an enthusiastic builder and he is reputed to have further developed parts of the town and added a chapel to the Manor House.

Woodstock seems to have been a favourite country residence of Queen Philippa of Haimault. In June 1330 she gave birth here to her first son who was later to become the Black Prince. During this time the Court was in residence at Woodstock for almost a third of the year. The Manor by then would have resembled more of a

*Blenheim Palace*

defensive castle than a Manor and probably had exterior walls with inner courtyards.

During this period in Woodstock's development it is worth mentioning Chaucer, the first of all English poets and author of *Canterbury Tales*. It has been claimed for generations that he was a 'local lad' who was born in the town. Unfortunately it seems more likely that he was born in London, the son of a vintner, but since Henry III spent so much time here Chaucer undoubtedly visited Woodstock frequently. He travelled abroad quite often on behalf of His Majesty and was thought well of by the King, so much so that he was given a pension for the work he had carried out. It is interesting to note that in Park Street, quite close to the entrance to Blenheim, the last house on the right is named Chaucer's House. It is generally thought that this house stands on the site of a former 15th century dwelling which in fact belonged to Chaucer's son, Thomas.

Throughout history Woodstock had been dependent on the Royal family's presence and the close proximity of Oxford. During the Civil War it was naturally a Royalist town. Immediately after the war and due to government by the Parliamentarians the town went into steep decline. The former Royal estate was neglected, the timber of the great forests was sold as were the deer that had previously been plentiful in the forest. There was no more coming and going of nobles with all the trimmings, the pomp and the retinues which previously had been the very reason for the town's development. The old palace was so badly damaged by the Cromwellian artillery during the 20 day siege that what was left of it was little more than a ruin. It was later demolished on the orders of Sarah, the first Duchess of Marlborough, in 1715 and today a stone marker close to the Grand Bridge in Blenheim Park is all that is left of this once historic building.

In 1704 Woodstock ceased to be a royal manor for the property was conferred on John Churchill, the first Duke of Marlborough, as a reward by a grateful nation for his tremendous and historic victory over Louis IV at Blenheim. From then on the town became of secondary importance and its well-being was to a great extent dictated by the new residents of The Palace.

The Palace of Blenheim took over 20 years to build and cost a huge amount of money at the time, probably more than £300,000. It was designed by John Vanbrugh and Nicholas Hawksmoor and at its conclusion covered seven acres. It was finished in 1725 and most certainly had a resemblance to the Palace of Versailles, which stood as a symbol of the quite arrogant monarch of France whose European, and indeed world ambitions had been curtailed on the battlefield of Blenheim in Bavaria on 13th August 1704.

Vanbrugh had led a most unusual life for an architect at that time or indeed at any other time. His grandfather Van Brugg was a Protestant from Ghent but Vanbrugh was brought up near the city of Chester. As a young man he served as an officer in the infantry but later turned to writing comedy plays. He became very confident, developing a certain style, and was thought of as a very imaginative fellow. Whilst he brimmed with ideas when, at 41 years of age, he was offered the commission to create his greatest work, he lacked the ability to communicate his ideas in a practical manner. This is where Nicholas Hawksmoor came in. He had studied under Wren and was an excellent draughtsman and designer and so it was that he and Vanbrugh go down in history as being an ideal combined team who eventually produced one of the most elaborate buildings in Europe and beyond, and certainly one of the finest examples of

English Baroque architecture. The Palace was built of stone from Taynton near Burford and it houses a breathtaking collection of fine furniture, paintings, tapestries and sculpture. The library alone is a room of 183ft in length housing over 10,000 volumes.

The Palace was the birthplace of Sir Winston Churchill and today the room in which he was born is open to the public. Also on show are a collection of his personal belongings, books, photographs and letters together with some of his paintings.

*Blenheim Palace, the Baroque Garden front*

In the grounds is the Marlborough Maze, the world's largest symbolic hedge maze which was opened to the public in 1991. The lake, the home of many varied waterfowl, and the 2,000 acres of parkland was Capability Brown's contribution to this fine estate during the late 18th century.

It is almost as if history has completed a full circle at Woodstock for throughout history the town existed because of the Royal Manor's close proximity and today the visitors in the main visit Woodstock because of Blenheim Palace's existence, the town, as before, providing accommodation, food, drink, lodging and souvenirs for

*Left:* Column of Victory, Blenheim Park
*Below:* Blenheim Park

visitors from all parts of the globe. Woodstock though has not become gaudy; the service it provides for the visitor is, if anything, discrete. It is not a large town but one which still retains a certain dignity of its own. It is a pleasant mixture of architectural styles from different periods of history and straddles the road from Oxford to Stratford-on-Avon. Solid stone buildings, public houses and hotels such as the Marlborough Arms in Oxford Street, The Bear in Park Street and The Feathers in Market Street mingle well with a variety of small shops to give a mixture of sophistication and attractiveness. Woodstock is also one of the few

places left in this country where gloves are still manufactured.

The town is not generally associated with horticulture but across the River Glyme is the lesser known village of Old Woodstock where, on the left up the hill, a plaque on a cottage wall tells of the original Blenheim Orange apple being raised in the garden of George Kempster, a tailor of Old Woodstock, who died in 1773.

The tower of the parish church stands proudly overlooking Park Street facing the stocks and the Oxford County Library just across the road. St. Mary Magdalene's has unfortunately been subjected to

*St Mary Magdalene church, Woodstock*

considerable refurbishment during the 19th century and little of the older building is evident. Originally the church for the town residents was at Bladon, where Sir Winston Churchill is buried. However, since it was a couple of miles to travel to Bladon a Chapel of Ease was built here but all that is left of it today is a small piece of the south wall and the Norman doorway with its chevron and roll mouldings around the arch and down the sides. During the 13th century the church was enlarged and it is quite possible that a chantry chapel was founded about 1210 by King John. Within 70 years the church is known to have had a grave yard and a bell tower. The south nave arcade and the south aisle date from around the same period and are some of the very few parts of the church which have remained unchanged since then. The eastern windows which have a quatrefoil piercing to the head of the stone at the window's head are also original, as are the arcades which have circular piers with a variety of heads carved into the capitals amidst detailed foliage. (On the third pillar the head with the silly face is said to depict Henry III.)

The church's font is 14th century while the attractive west porch was constructed about a century later. During the Civil War the church was damaged by the Parliamentarians but later in 1686 the Bishop of Oxford paid for the Rectory to be built so that the Rector could then reside amongst his flock. This stone building is now a private residence known as the Bishop's House and overlooks Blenheim Park, the new rectory being completed in 1982.

During the late 18th century much rebuilding and enlarging took place on the tower and the north aisle with the addition of a gallery. A century later the north aisle

was rebuilt and a vestry and Lady Chapel were added. In 1953 the equipment that operates the daily chimes (the chimes play different tunes every four hours, seven days a week) was restored to commemorate the Quincentenary of the Borough; donations were received toward the cost from over 40 towns and villages in different parts of the world, all with the name of Woodstock.

Despite the continual modification and rebuilding the church, whilst not being one of the most famous in the Cotswolds, is certainly a very pleasant one and still retains a fair mixture of memorial windows and tablets. Of the latter perhaps the most unusual is the memorial to James King who was a companion to Captain Cook who discovered Australia. James King was the son of a clergyman from Lancashire and at the tender age of 12 years he joined the navy. Fourteen years later he was serving aboard the *Resolution* as second lieutenant. He was a very intelligent young man who had studied astronomy and proved to be a quick and efficient officer on Cook's third voyage. In 1775 he succeeded to the command of *Discovery* and it was he who assisted in the preparation of Captain Cook's journal. Unfortunately he was only 34 years old when he died.

Close by the church is Garret House where the town clerk, Edmund Hiorne, resided at the time of the Civil War. It was he who surrendered the town armour to the Royalists and consequently was dragged before Parliament to beg forgiveness before being removed from office in 1646.

The nearby and aptly named village of Stonesfield is where the stone was quarried to refurbish the buildings at Woodstock during and after the construction of Blenheim Palace. Much false fronting was done to older timber frame dwellings while other houses were pulled down and completely rebuilt. It seems as if a wave of change came over the town since reaching what was probably its lowest ebb immediately following the Civil War. With the construction of Blenheim Palace the town seemed to enter a new era with a certain vigour. For instance The Bear Hotel, probably the oldest hotel in Woodstock, is said to date from medieval times but from the outside you would hardly think so due to the updating which took place during this era.

At the head of Park Street stands the 18th century Town Hall with its council chamber raised on arches above the market place, the arches only being built in 1888. At the opposite end of the street is the

*The Town Hall, Woodstock*

Triumphal Arch of Blenheim Park, beyond which the landscaping of Capability Brown enhances the view up to the Palace itself.

The successive Dukes of Marlborough had been little interested in the townsfolk or in the development of the town, but they had pursued their own interest in local agricultural development with some vigour. The glove making industry during this time received no help or encouragement to expand further than that of a cottage industry based on its outworkers. The fourth Duke however was very enthusiastic about the development of canals which during the late 1700s and until the development of the railways became this country's major trade routes. In 1802 it was felt that the river from Charlbury to the Thames at Cassington could be made navigable and this would provide transport facilities to the west of Blenheim Park. In the event only a short stretch of canal was completed, but cargoes of salt, lime and coal amongst other commodities were transported on the new system for the Blenheim estates. Woodstock and its surrounding traders however used road transport to reach the offloading wharfs of Cassington, Eynsham or Thrupp.

At this time the town was frequently and regularly served by a stage coach network, with coaches calling regularly at The Bear, The Star and The Marlborough Arms Hotels. The town of course was well positioned between Shipston-on-Stour, Stratford-on-Avon and Oxford and by the early 1800s Woodstock had become a coaching town. Consequently many local people found employment as innkeepers, stablemen, grooms or servants.

By 1840 the Great Western Railway Company had opened up a route between Steventon and Reading and 42 years later the then Duke of Marlborough had offered land for a branch line between Woodstock and Woodstock Road Station just a few

miles distant. Whether or not the reason was for the convenience of the Churchill family or a genuine desire to help the town seems unclear but eventually during the life of the Eighth Duke, the father of Sir Winston, moves were afoot to construct the desired branch line.

The Woodstock Branch railway line was opened in 1890. It was intended that it should run along the eastern edge of the Oxfordshire Cotswolds for less than 4 miles. It was quite simple in its conception and quite simple in its scale, for it started life with no grandiose ideas, merely that it should serve the townsfolk and the local villagers and carry local people and produce. Sadly it remained part of the local scene for barely 64 years and is now only remembered by those 'locals' of more advanced years of life. During this time in Woodstock glove making formed a large part of the local industry. Vast numbers of poorly paid out-workers painstakingly sewed gloves in their own living rooms for a mere pittance. On sunny days, so it was said, female craft workers would sit at their cottage doors while their menfolk would work at preparing the raw sheepskins, stretching and bleaching the skins in and around the open areas of the town. Thus it was that the vast majority of the labouring classes of the town earned their keep by the production of gloves for the fair hands of the ladies of Oxford, London and beyond. The railway in its early days carried out the gloves in great hampers, which in addition to farm, agriculture and coal produce was the basis of the railway's cargo!

The railway unfortunately was a shortsighted and short lived success. It survived for a few short years and died a drawn out death. In its heyday it had promised to be the great opening of a new era in transport technology in this perhaps forgotten part of rural Oxfordshire, but in reality it became a short lived wonder. The route, like so many of the canal routes before it, was ill thought out and poorly conceived and in this new age of steam the Woodstock Branch joined too late. Technology had bypassed it, road surfaces had improved and the internal combustion engine was developing steadily. Today there is very little evidence left of this 'local' railway's existence but the small terminus station is still standing just past the junction of Oxford Street and the High Street and today is used as a garage. It certainly seems to have been a railway line having a strong connection with Woodstock and with the town's former Royal romantic connections of yesteryear; for the regular Woodstock branch engine was numbered 1473 and in 1896 she was named *Fair Rosamund*.

*The Bear Inn, Woodstock*

## WOODSTOCK

| | |
|---|---|
| P | Parking |
| T | Toilets |
| 1 | Church of St. Mary Magdalene |
| 2 | Town Hall |
| 3 | Triumphal Arch |
| 4 | Chaucer's House |
| 5 | Stocks |
| 6 | Bear Hotel |
| 7 | Museum |

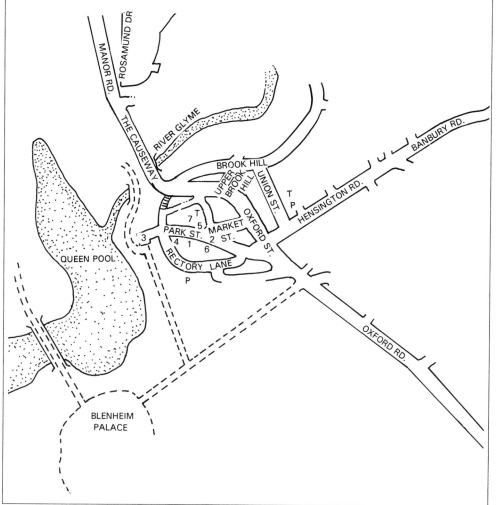

# 20: Wotton-under-Edge

*The Berkeley House, Long Street*

There are very few extremes of architecture in Wotton. Most of the buildings are of agreeable proportions dating from the late 17th and 18th centuries. About the centre of this country town many of the ground floors of the former houses of merchants and clothiers have, over the centuries, been changed into shop fronts. Compared with most of the other towns in this book Wotton is perhaps less visited by tourists and more worked in by its residents.

On this western edge of the steep sided Cotswolds the town, which was previously part of the estate of Berkeley, sits at the entrance to Tyle Bottom and to the east and to the north the woods and copses brush close to its very edges.

Way back in AD940 King Edmund of Wessex, who was the grandson of Alfred the Great, leased four hides of land to Theign Edric. Wotton at that time was called Wudetun. There is evidence to suggest that there had been settlements in the vicinity during earlier periods in history but this Saxon record is the only written proof. However, a coin of the Roman Emperor Galienus, together with part of a Roman spoon, both found locally, indicate that there was certainly a Roman presence in the area. Indeed excavations close to Ashel Barn in recent years have revealed the existence of a sizeable Romano British settlement close to the boundary of the parish.

Following the departure of the Romans the Saxons came and after the Battle of Dynham in AD577, there followed a gradual arrival of Saxon peoples, many coming from further north. The surrounding areas eventually became a part of the sub-kingdom of Hwiccia which was ruled by King Penda of Mercia.

Wudetun was known as a settlement in woodland and it probably consisted of a series of huts and farm buildings close to a plentiful water supply from the Edbrooke. Following the death of King Penda the Pagan in AD654, monks from Lindisfarne arrived in middle England and later established themselves at Malmesbury and Tetbury from where it is probable that missionaries ventured out amongst those whom they aimed to convert within the Wotton area.

By 1086 the Normans mentioned Wotton as Vuntune in the Domesday Survey. It was one small part of the huge manor of Berkeley, previously owned by Edward the Confessor but following the Battle of Hastings William the Conqueror gave it to Roger, one of his barons. At nearby Dursley, Roger had a simple motte and bailey fortress constructed. This was later superseded by a stone building and the castle at Berkeley was also founded around this time. From then on the various Earls of Berkeley and their offspring ruled the Manor of "Wuttun" throughout most of the Middle Ages. After part of the town was sacked during King John's reign following the baronial revolt, Jane de Somery established an annual fair and a weekly market in 1252. By 1273 the town gained the status of a Borough, with a mayor, a dozen Aldermen, a mace bearer and a couple of constables. Her reasons for such development were of course purely selfish, although it was hailed as a major step forward for the masses. It was never intended that the people of the town should benefit but that these developments should attract the richer merchant families from other parts of the Cotswolds and indeed from even further afield. For if these people settled at Wotton then of course she and her family would benefit from whatever taxable dealings were carried out by them. Similarly those folk who now held stalls at the weekly markets were likewise required to pay for this facility. Additionally a toll was levied on each transaction which took place.

From the 13th century Wotton's main source of income was from the cloth making and weaving trades and as elsewhere, the bulk of the work was carried out, literally, as numerous small cottage industries. The Cotswold area including Wotton was booming. The town's buildings at this time would have been in the main timber framed with an infill of lath and plaster, probably with thatched roofs although as time went on those who could afford it added a roof of Cotswold stone slivers or tiles. During later centuries old timberwork has been revealed in premises in the High Street and in Long Street when façades have been added to older properties in order to update them.

For a town of modest size, compared with other Cotswold towns of the period, it is interesting to note that a free grammar school with a school house was in existence at Wotton as early as 1291. It is most unlikely that anyone, other than the sons of the rich, would be allowed to attend, nevertheless it was thought to have been one of the earliest schools in existence in the country. This initial early start to educate at Wotton was followed in 1348 by the Lady Berkeley endowing and providing a new house for a new school. This may have been the commencement of a larger enterprise or it could have been the continuation of the former school, it is not clear, but at that time the goodly Lady Berkeley endowed the school with a number of properties in the town and over 160 acres of land close by. The teacher was a priest of course and was required to celebrate mass each day before commencement of classes. He became known as the Morrow Mass priest. At this time two scholars from the poor of the town were also provided for. All students were to be age 10 years at commencement and were expected to continue their studies until the age of 16. In 1417 one of the town's strongest supporters, the fourth Thomas

*Left: The Town Hall*

*Right: The Old Tolsey with its elaborate clock on the corner of Market Street*

*Below: The Old Ram Inn*

Berkeley, who was at that time probably the richest member of the family, departed this life. He died in the manor house. His wife, the only daughter of Lord de Lisle, also died at Wotton. Their daughter later became the wife of Richard Beauchamp, Earl of Warwick, the most powerful earl in the country. It was not long before Elizabeth laid claim to all her father's estates. She greatly resented the fact that he had chosen to adopt an orphaned nephew and to leave any of his estates to him. Whilst this nephew was away Elizabeth and her husband seized Berkeley Castle and obtained from the King the

*The Falcon Inn*

right to hold all the manors until such time as the rightful inheritance dispute was settled. From this time the disputes as to the rightful ownership took almost 200 years, during which there were numerous outbreaks of violence and legal wrangling. The town itself suffered from these disputes frequently, the rioting flared up in the town and Wotton itself was damaged during this period on more than one occasion. A recorder of events at the time wrote that local villages had also been damaged and the countryside ravaged but little other mention of such activities is made in other documentation of the period.

After centuries of involvement in the wool trade certain people have stood out in Wotton just as they did in other Cotswold towns. Thomas Gower, a rich clothier, died in 1572 leaving a considerable amount of money to his immediate family. In addition to his business interests at Wotton he had spinners and weavers in the surrounding towns and through his generosity the poor of these towns were also to benefit from his legacies.

During the early 1600s the Venn family were wealthy and became famous, one of the sons travelling to London and developing a successful haberdashery business, later becoming an Alderman of the City. He purchased land at nearby Nibly and made a present of a pair of large silver flagons to St. Mary's church. Finally he benefited the town by providing a water source at the Market Cross.

The son of Thomas Perry, also a clothier of the town, was Hugh who eventually became a committee member of the East India Company. His bequests to the town included the building of the almshouses in Church Street and the provision of clothing and income to 12 old men and women.

By the year 1600 the Little Avon and its tributaries had around 18 mills working along the river banks. Frequently two

different processes were carried out side by side, corn milling and fulling making use of the same water source. At the same time almost 30 clothiers carried on their business in Wotton and the surrounding villages, while there must have been around 100 weavers and apprentice weavers at that time. The resultant broadcloth was sold mostly in an undyed state while some was finished and dyed before shipment. Most of the cloth was transported to the capital city by a regular group of carriers who were town residents. The central "staging post" or terminus for these haulage wagons was at Smiths Shop, later known as Hunters Hall. Coventry, in the Midlands, was another outlet for Wotton broadcloth with the finishing and dyeing also being carried out there.

As the 1600s progressed the quality of the cloth being produced was improving. Credit for this is usually given to the arrival at Wotton of weavers from the Low Countries and to the skills of the Huguenot immigrants who escaped from persecution in France. At this time the best of English cloth was made from Hereford sheep which produced a shorter and less coarse wool. Later the Spanish Merino wool was imported, from which a finer and lighter cloth could be manufactured. This was a tremendous improvement on the traditional Cotswold broadcloth. The development of this product in England was much influenced by a Wotton man, Benedict Webb of Kingswood, who travelled to France in order to learn the methods being used there. Armed with this new knowledge he returned to England and settled first at Taunton in Somerset, later moving back to Wotton and spreading the new knowledge for this process to Uley, Stroud and Dursley. The Civil War and the fighting with the Dutch obviously affected the growth of the industry, nevertheless the development of further markets abroad meant that Wotton prospered well into the 17th century.

As mentioned in my opening paragraphs, the older parts of today's town date mainly from this period and from the 18th century. The Berkeley House, gabled and Jacobean, and the Falcon Hotel, both in Long Street, are from the same period. The Falcon is dated 1659. By the early 1700s Carlton House also stood in the same street and marked a change in architectural styles, with its symmetrical façades, fanlighted doors and, typical of the period which followed, large sash windows. A little later the Old Rectory had a Georgian false front

added by Thomas Rous. It is today one of the town's most handsome houses; known as The Court it stands in Culverhay. Just across the street Edbrooke House was originally owned by the Venn family. It was bought from them by Thomas Rous who probably built its imposing façade of three storeys with the Doric doorway.

Near the junction of Potters Pond and School Road is the old Grammar School built in 1726. Today's school is on Kingswood Road. The oldest building in Wotton is probably the Ram Inn which may date from as early as 1350 and was probably originally the home of a priest.

*Gateway to Perry and Dawes Almshouses*

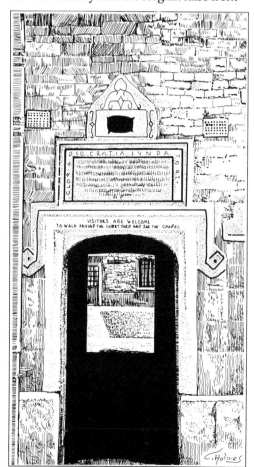

*Perry and Dawes Almshouses in Church Street*

Possibly the best known of Wotton's architecture stands in Church Street where Hugh Perry made provision for the construction of his almshouses. In 1712 Thomas Dawes provided for additions to be made and when, a little later, the old almshouses in Culverhay were pulled down to provide space for the new Blue Coat School, the Perry and Dawes buildings were further extended. Here the visitor should go through the entrance below the plaque commemorating their construction in 1638 and where the message on the lintel reads: "Visitors are welcome to walk round the courtyard and to see the chapel." Inside is a

small grass quadrangle and the delightful tiny chapel.

The town's other almshouses are of much more recent construction. Those opposite the church were founded in 1837 by Ann Beanpacker and 50 years later the Rev. Rowland Hill provided for the almshouses at the top of Old Town.

Many of the dwellings in the High Street were false fronted and provided with Georgian façades during the late 1700s. Occasionally an extra storey was also added. At the corner of Market Street, the old Tolsey House is such an example. It was originally given to the town by the Countess

131

of Warwick in 1595 and served as the Court of Piepowder. The court was set up to deal with offences concerning the travelling traders, being those people with "dusty feet" or "pieds poudrés", and all other manner of market traders' disputes and taxes. Today it is recognisable by its handsome weather vane in the form of a dragon which surmounts its bell turret, not to mention the large Victorian Jubilee clock which hangs over the pavement.

Wotton-Under-Edge rose in prosperity when the need for wool products increased and when the markets waned, then the residents of Wotton tightened their belts.

From the early 1790s the conflicts in France affected the industry and it was not until after the Duke of Wellington defeated the French at Waterloo over 20 years later that the business settled down again. During these stop-start years of warfare large quantities of cloth were required for army uniforms, both for those battalions sent to fight overseas and for the increasing number of militia who were recruited, just as the home guard was raised during the Second World War to repel an invasion of these islands while our main forces were engaged elsewhere.

The decline on the other hand started around 1800 when various inventions introduced into the woollen and weaving trades reduced the need for hand labour and speeded up the manufacturing process. The development of the spinning jenny is perhaps the best known of these. By the early 1800s steam engines were operating in the Wotton mills and by 1835 broadcloth was being woven by the power loom. Competitive markets added to the problems of the mill owners and the workers alike but all in all trouble brewed at Wotton, strikes resulted from unrest and some mills became insolvent. By the mid 1800s larger mills with smaller work forces were producing more cloth. As the industrial revolution developed in other parts of England, the Cotswolds including Wotton was by-passed, thus we have what we see today and are grateful for it!

No visit to Wotton would be complete without looking in at the Tabernacle. This 19th century neo-Gothic structure houses a reproduction of the world famous Woodchester pavement together with specimens recovered from the Roman settlement at close by Kingscote.

Finally, the town's church. Dedicated to St. Mary the Virgin it dates from the 13th century and has an 11th century Perpendicular Gothic tower. The south

porch with its sun dial has an interior doorway from the 13th century, above which is a priest's chamber. Inside and much restored during the last century the church has wide aisles and white walls, thus it gives an exceptional impression of spaciousness. The organ, which was built for George I as a gift for London's St. Martin in the Fields, was played upon by Handel and is certainly one of the church's proudest possessions. Other items of value include the full size brasses on top of the 15th century tomb of the 10th Lord and Lady Berkeley. These are considered to be amongst the finest of that period in England. At the sanctuary entrance hangs a two tier, twelve armed chandelier in brass, which was given to the church in 1763 by William Moore.

*Below: St Mary's Church*
*Below right: Old porch of the church of St Mary's*

**WOTTON-UNDER-EDGE**

P    Parking
P.O. Post Office
T    Toilets
1    Church of St. Mary the Virgin
2    The Ann Beanpacker Almshouses
3    The former Ram Inn
4    Perry and Dawes Almshouses
5    Berkeley House
6    Town Hall
7    Tolsey House
8    Sir Isaac Pitman's House

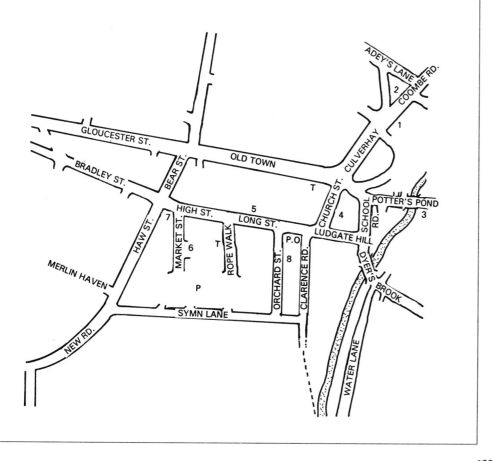

# Bibliography

*A Portrait of Winchcombe.* D.N. Donaldson. Published at 56 Gretton Road Winchcombe Glous. 1978

*The Official Guide to Winchcombe.* Winchcombe & District Chamber of Trade & Commerce. Second Edition

*Winchcombe Cavalcade.* E. Adlard. J. Burrow & Co. 1939

*Hailes Abbey.* D. Winkless. Spredden Press. 1990

*Sudeley Castle.* M. Roulstone. Garrod Status. 1974

*Hailes Abbey.* J.G. Coad. English Heritage. 1993

*The Book of Campden.* G. Powell. Barracuda Books. 1982

*A History of Chipping Norton.* E. Meades. Bodkin. 1984

*Historic Towns in Gloucestershire.* R. Leech Craags. Mark Lane. Bristol. 1981

*Stow-On-The-Wold.* J. Johnson. Alan Sutton Publishing. 1994

*Bourton-On-The-Water.* T. Wray & D. Stratford. Alan Sutton Publishing. 1994

*The Book of Burford.* R.& J. Moody. Barracuda Books. 1983

*Burford Past and Present.* M.S. Gretton. Faber & Faber. 1944

*Buildings of the Cotswolds.* D. Moriarty. Victor Gollanoz. 1989

*The Cotswolds.* R. Witeman. Weidenfeld & Nicolson. 1987

*Cotswold Heritage.* L. Wright & J. Priddey. Robert Hale. 1977

*The Cotswolds.* H. Newbury. Country Life Books. 1982

*The Spirit of the Cotswolds.* S. Hill. Michael Joseph. 1988

*The Buildings of England. Gloucestershire, The Cotswolds.* N. Pevsner-D. Verey. Penguin Books.1979

*Gloucester. A History & Guide.* C. Heighway. Alan Sutton Publishing. 1985

*Cheltenham.* Town & County Books. 1983

*Cirencester. Capital Of The Cotswolds.* Cirencester Town Council

*History of Tetbury.* E. Hodgson. Alan Sutton Publishing.1976

*Introduction to Woodstock.* J.M. Shelmerdine. Samson Press 1951

*The Woodstock Branch.* R. Lingard. Oxford Publishing Co. 1973

*The Woodstock Branch.* S.C. Jenkins. Wild Swan Publications. 1987

*Bourton On The Water.* T. Wray & D. Stratford. Alan Sutton Publishing. 1994

*Oxfordshire & Berkshire.* R. Lethbridge. Michael Joseph. 1988

*Blenheim Revisited.* Hugh Montgomery Massingbred. Bodley Head. 1985

*Blenheim Biography of a Palace.* M. Fowler. Penguin Books. 1989

*Introduction to Woodstock.* J.M. Shelmerdine. Samson Press. 1951

*A Short History of Moreton-In-Marsh.* W.L. Warne. Journal Press 1948

*The Cotswold Town of Moreton-In-Marsh, Gloucester, England.* Corsham Publishing, Corsham, Wilts.

*The Book of Cheltenham.* S. Blake & R. Beacham. Barracuda Books. 1982

*A History of Cheltenham.* G. Hart. Leicester University Press.1965

*A guide to Chipping Norton & its Cotswold Countryside.* Chipping Norton & District Chamber of Trade & Commerce. 1994

*Portrait of The Cotswolds.* E. Brill. Robert Hale. 1964

*Beatrix Potter's Gloucester.* K. Clark. F. Warne & Co. 1988

*Gloucester Cathedral.* J. Wilton-Smith. Pitkin Pictorials. 1994

*The Battle of Tewkesbury.* W.D. Pereira. Line One Pub. 1983

*Tewkesbury.* A. Jones. Phillimore & Co. 1987

*Parish Church of St. Mary, Cheltenham.* Canon G.W. Hart

*A History of Malmesbury.* Dr. Bernulf Hodge. Friends of Malmesbury Abbey, printed Taylor & Sons Minety

*Malmesbury Town Guide.* Official Civic Publications.

*A Picture Book of Malmesbury.* Muriel Beak. M.L. Beak, High St. Malmesbury

*Painswick. The Official Guide.* Published under the authority of the Parish Council. 1984

*The City of Bath.* R.W.M. Wright and G. Lester. Pitkin Pictorials. 1973

*City of Gloucester.* Gilbert Thurlow. Pitkin Pictorials.1981

*The City of Bath.* Barry Cunliffe. Alan Sutton. 1986

*The City of Bath.* Photographs by Colin Baxter. Colin Baxter Photography, Lanark.1990

*Bath and its Surroundings.* Photos by Neil Gibson. Moonracker Press. 1975

*Historic Gloucester.* Philip Moss. The Windrush Press. 1993

*Cirencester. A History and Guide.* Jean Welsford. Alan Sutton. 1987

*Cirencester. The official Town Guide.* The British Publishing Company.

*Bath.* J. Haddon. B.T. Batsford. 1973.

*Bath. The Colour Souvenir Guide.* P. Newman. Pevensey Press. 1986

*The Dream of Bath.* D. Winsor. Trade & Trade Publications. 1984

*Wool & Water.* K.G. Ponting. Moonraker Press. 1975.

*Bradford on Avon. A History To 1950.* W.R. Powell. Wiltshire County Council. 1990

*Bradford on Avon Past and Present.* H. Fassnidge. Ex. Libris Press. 1993

*Minchinhampton and Avening.* A.T. Playne. Alan Sutton.1978

*Minchinhampton Local History Folder.* Minchinhampton Library

*Minchinhampton & District Official Guide.* Minchinhampton Parish Council. Fourth Edition

*Wotton under Edge. Offical Guide.* D. Milner. Town Council. 1986

*Wotton under Edge. Times Past.* R. Perry. Panes Associates. 1988

*Wotton under Edge.* E.S. Lindley. Alan Sutton.1977

*Under the Hill.* S. Herrick. Alan Sutton. 1979

*Edward II, Suddenly at Berkeley.* R. Perry. Ivy House Books.1988